N

# When Marxists
# Do Research

# When Marxists Do Research

**Pauline Marie Vaillancourt**

CONTRIBUTIONS IN POLITICAL SCIENCE, NUMBER 150

GREENWOOD PRESS
NEW YORK
WESTPORT, CONNECTICUT
LONDON

**Library of Congress Cataloging-in-Publication Data**

Vaillancourt, Pauline Marie.
   When Marxists do research.

   (Contributions in political science, ISSN 0147–1066 ;
no. 150)
   Bibliography: p.
   Includes index.
   1. Social science—Research.  2. Communism and
philosophy.  3. Knowledge, Theory of.  I. Title.
II. Series.
H61.V27  1986      300'.72      85–27254
ISBN 0–313–24703–X (lib. bdg. : alk. paper)

Library of Congress Catalog Card Number: 85–27254
ISBN: 0–313–24703–X
ISSN: 0147–1066

First published in 1986

Greenwood Press, Inc.
88 Post Road West, Westport, Connecticut 06881

Printed in the United States of America

The paper used in this book complies with the
Permanent Paper Standard issued by the National
Information Standards Organization (Z39.48–1984).

10 9 8 7 6 5 4 3 2 1

This book is dedicated to those who I wish had been here to
read it and scold me about its contents

Ivan Joseph Kubanis
San Diego State University
A principled teacher
1921–67

Walter D. Young
University of Victoria
A principled colleague
1933–84

# CONTENTS

# TABLES

# PREFACE

A preface serves a number of different purposes. First, it gives one a chance to thank those who have assisted the author in one way or another during the period when he or she was writing the book. Second, it provides an opportunity for the author to communicate to the reader what motivated him or her to write the book. Third, it offers a chance to fend off criticism and confess sins before adept reviewers of the book perform this task. Finally, it provides the author with a chance to add any important afterthoughts.

Many people should be thanked for assistance in the writing of this book. David Braybrook, Harry Bredemeier, and Edmund Mokrzycki were kind enough to read the manuscript and make comments on it. The person who deserves the most acknowledgment and who spent a number of days, if not weeks, going over the manuscript and offering comments has declined to receive any public recognition of his contribution, asking only that I thank the "anonymous reviewer." This I do without reservation. My "anonymous reviewer" takes this position because he seems to think that the kind of contribution he has made here constitutes a "normal professional responsibility." He believes that those with knowledge have an obligation to share what they know and to assist others without expecting recognition or compensation beyond a simple thank you. This book would in all probability never have been written without his help, criticism, encouragement, and (despite the fact that he does not believe in it in principle) even a small measure of praise from time to time. All of this was necessary, and all of it is acknowledged and appreciated. Neither he nor anyone other than the author can be held responsible for the final product, however.

Appreciation is extended to Ann Rajan-Gamina who juggled a range of tasks related to the production of this book with competence and good spirits. Greenwood Production Editor Arlene Belzer is commended for her helpful comments and her patience. Alix Evrard, University of Quebec-Montreal library staff member, was exceptionally aggressive and diligent in seeking out research materials on inter-library loan.

A word of thanks also goes to both the University of Quebec at Montreal and the Social Sciences and Humanities Research Council of Canada which provided grants for this project.

The motivation for writing this book comes out of my own rather unusual professional experience. Trained to do research as required by the norms of contemporary social science in what is considered to be one of the best political science departments in North America, I found myself in another country, attempting to teach social science methodology in a foreign language to university students who, for the most part, were either Marxists of one variety or another or sympathetic to Marxism. This book is the result of the discussions and confrontations associated with that experience.

Thanks, too, must go to colleagues at this same university, principally in the Political Science Department, many of them Marxists themselves, who were so patient with an American who was certainly ill-prepared for the tasks she assumed. I have learned much from them over the years about both the strengths and the weaknesses of a Marxist point of view.

It would take a volume equal to or greater than that which awaits the reader to adequately ward off criticism and confess all my "sins" when the topic involves something as controversial as Marxism and research. I will begin with a note on method. The reader will at once be aware that the conclusions reached in this book do not meet the standards of rigorous inquiry set for the Marxists whose research is being evaluated. My method is that of description and evaluation. I have no pretensions about offering rigorously tested knowledge here, though many of these generalizations about Marxist research could be subject to such testing. The questions considered require systematic research but are so numerous and far-reaching as to make it a monumental undertaking to do so. This being the case, I can only underline the tentative character of the views set out here.

Another "sin" to be acknowledged in this preface is that complicated epistemological and methodological questions are presented in an oversimplified manner in this book. The reader is reminded that the intended audience is not the philosopher but the practicing non-Marxist social scientist. Simplification and popularization facilitate communication of complicated information about how Marxists do research to the intended audience. In addition, a relatively stereotyped, yes, even mechanical view of social research goes unquestioned, for the most part, throughout the book. This is because so many social scientists today accept this model, but its use also reflects my own view that such a model is not wholly without merit, though it is certainly open to improvement.

Finally, some afterthoughts are in order. In writing this book I learned that Marxist views of research are mixed and sometimes even antagonistic. The founding fathers of Marxism were not always consistent. Sometimes they employed empirical modes of inquiry, but at other times they expressed serious doubts about it. The ambiguity and contradiction in their writings have, over the years, permitted selective and divergent interpretations. As will be seen in the pages that follow, a number of very different, but all legitimately Marxist, views of research resulted.

In this book I argue that one group of Marxists, which I call the materialist Marxists, does research much as required by the norms of contemporary social science. Given this standard of judgment the materialists are repeatedly found to be more successful than the other groups studied on almost all the research-related questions discussed. If other questions had been asked, the results might have been different. Certainly there is much to criticize about the materialist Marxists such as their opportunism and their lack of principle when in power. This line of argument is not developed in this book because the concern here is limited to questions related to inquiry.

Since the materialist Marxists do research much as required by modern non-Marxist social science conventions, the reader may, understandably, ask whether or not they are really Marxists at all! The answer to the question is yes, they are still Marxists. What distinguishes them from non-Marxists is not their assumptions about epistemology, method, or science, how they do research, how they defend their knowledge claims, or how they produce policy. Rather, their identity as Marxists is dependent on specific substantive views they hold about humankind and society which are usually associated with a Marxist point of view. The materialist Marxists share with some, though not all, other Marxists a belief that equality and collective rights are more important than personal liberty and individual rights. They emphasize, at least in theory, equitable social relations. They have a whole set of beliefs about institutional arrangements which are quite different from those preferred and observed in non-socialist countries, for example, the superiority of public ownership.

The materialists adopt the research strategies and the research techniques of modern social science because their intellectual point of reference is a Marxist tradition that emphasizes the value of concrete inquiry. This tradition is different from that recognized by other Marxists. The materialists are inspired by the legacy in Marxism which emphasizes the importance of rigorous, testable research. They are influenced by the research example of Marx, Engels, Lenin, and Mao. They are the successors to the Marx who drew up the sociological questionnaire published in the *Socialist Review* in France (Marx, 1880), and who was fascinated by mathematics (Gerdes, 1985) as well as to the Engels who wrote *Condition of the Working Class in England* (1969). They look to the Mao who emphasized systematic research in his essays "Against Book Worship" and "Preface to *Rural Surveys*" (Mao, 1971). They are influenced by the Lenin who wrote *Development of Capitalism in Russia* (Lenin, 1956), by his suggestion that statistical data are "precise and indisputable" when taken in "their entirety, in their interconnection," by his insistence that data "are not only stubborn things, but undoubtedly proof-bearing things" (Lenin, 1964:272–73), and by his example when he came to power of setting up the Socialist Academy of Social Sciences to carry out research and the Central Statistical Board to collect data, administer questionnaires and do interviews (Weinberg, 1974:6–7; Szacki, 1979:32; Lewin, 1974:116). The goal of these agencies was to provide the new revolutionary government with information such as inventories pertinent for making decisions (Matthews, 1978; Larionov, 1970:84–85).

The fact that the materialist Marxists do research much as required by the norms of contemporary social science has important implications for how they view Marxism itself. This point is not discussed in this book, but it is worthy of note.

The materialist Marxists' assumptions about inquiry and the way they do research and make policy permit them to reintroduce the importance of evidence and testing into Marxism; and require that they define Marxism as open and subject to correction. It is no surprise that there is a general consensus among the materialists that many of Marx's theories can and should be subject to rigorous and systematic study and tested against evidence (Szczepanski, 1966:46). The materialists propose refinements to Marxist theory based on evidence in an effort to improve and update it. They strive for "a Marxism which generates propositions about the real world which can be empirically studied" (Wright, 1978: 10). They aim to develop a research agenda based in Marxian concepts and theories. Because their research practice includes the application and correction of theory and policy, it encourages them to build a learning component into Marxism itself, increasing the probability of correcting mistakes, profiting from experience, and producing new Marxist theory in the future.

The way the materialists do research and make policy discourages dogmatism and sectarianism both in the West and in the socialist countries (Bottomore, 1978) because it requires that judgment be based not on abstract principles so much as on concrete results. Their research practice militates against the "ossification of Marxism into a set of scholastic and dogmatic principles" (Goode, 1979:156). Political orthodoxy and intellectual purity have no role to play.

Were the materialist Marxists more numerous and more influential within Marxism, today and in the past, the body of Marxist research of interest to non-Marxists would probably be substantially greater. In fact, there are certain signs that the kind of pragmatism the materialist Marxists represent is on the ascendancy. This is an additional reason why it is important to understand how they and other Marxists do research.

# 1.

## RESEARCH AND MARXISM

This is a book about one important intellectual and practical dimension of contemporary Marxism, an attempt to evaluate Marxist research. The central focus is on how different Marxist groups carry out social, political, and economic inquiry, in particular: the intellectual predispositions and assumptions they bring to their studies, the influence of these views on how they actually do research, the strategies and techniques they employ when they do research, and the value of the results of their studies for defending knowledge claims and for formulating reasoned policy to act on real world problems. The approach is critical or evaluative and not merely descriptive.

The book is written primarily with the non-Marxist reader in mind, avoiding specialized vocabulary and jargon as much as possible. I have tried to provide non-Marxists with a basic understanding of the various orientations within contemporary Marxism and with some appreciation for the quality and scope of their social research.

Why should non-Marxists take an interest in Marxist research? There are very good reasons to do so. Marxists possess a rich tradition, a body of experience, accumulated over a hundred years and more, which non-Marxists have for the most part ignored. Nearly half of the world's population lives under governments inspired by Marx and his successors. Marxists have initiated some of the more dramatic social experiments of our times, attempting to construct new social relationships and to establish innovative institutional arrangements. Vast populations have been mobilized; peasant societies have been rapidly modernized; forms of ownership have been transformed. Marxist research on these and related matters is potentially of great significance for everyone. Although the results of some of this research may not be generally accessible, much is available in articles published in journals, presented at international conferences, and so on.

No attempt is made here to review the substance of Marxist research. A certain number of such inventories already exist (Anderson, 1976 and 1984; Flacks and Turkel, 1978; Kesselman, 1983; Vaillancourt, 1979), and more are certainly needed. Rather, the purpose of this book is to assist non-Marxists to understand how individuals of different Marxist orientations undertake inquiry and to provide non-Marxists with a basis for proceeding if it appears that something can be learned from the way specific Marxist currents do research.

Assessing these matters is not an easy task because not all Marxists agree on the assumptions underlying research or on how it should be carried out. Indeed, the disagreements among them are a point of central concern here, for today there is a surprising heterogeneity of perspectives within Marxism on questions related to social science inquiry—epistemology, method, science, research, and knowledge generally. On some of these questions Marxists are intellectually closer to other non-Marxists who share their assumptions than they are to fellow Marxists with whom they disagree. Indeed, there is such diversity within Marxism on these matters that one wonders what makes Marxists and their inquiries distinctive. This question is important and was examined briefly in the preface, but a complete consideration of it goes well beyond the present work.

The approach to Marxist inquiry taken in Chapters 2 through 4 is first to set out the broad general assumptions that underlie inquiry and then to use this generally accepted model of inquiry as a basis for examining and comparing the implicit and explicit premises which the various Marxist groups make about research. What is referred to as the generally accepted model is employed because it summarizes the criteria of acceptability in *contemporary* social science for producing defensible knowledge and because, with the addition of a few elements, it satisfies the requirements for reasoned action or policymaking as they are accepted at the present time.

Marxist research-relevant assumptions will be compared with the requirements of the generally accepted model and described from three different perspectives: epistemology, methodology, and science. These three reference points were chosen because they make it possible to see what each of the various Marxist groups hopes to accomplish in undertaking research and because they permit significant differences between the Marxist orientations to be clearly identified. Taken together these three perspectives help us understand why Marxists choose particular research strategies and how they use specific research techniques. Examining epistemological premises draws attention to certain research-relevant aspects of Marxist inquiry. Looking at their views of methodology brings out additional information. Considering their understanding of science clarifies other features of the enterprise. All three are essential for an adequate evaluation; together they provide a fairly straightforward basis for assessment.

The choice of these perspectives (epistemology, methodology, and science) for considering Marxist assumptions about research is not without certain inconveniences. These concepts are not entirely distinct from each other. Nomenclature in these matters is not standard. Considering the same set of assumptions, the same substantive material, from these three perspectives inevitably involves overlap and a certain amount of repetition and redundancy from chapter to chapter. In addition, it is not always easy to isolate the views of the various Marxists on these questions because they do not always clearly articulate their underlying assumptions on these matters.

## ORGANIZATION OF THE BOOK

The plan for the remainder of this first chapter is (1) to lay out the material to be covered in each chapter of the book, (2) to outline in detail the generally accepted model and the policymaking model to be used for assessing Marxist assumptions about research, and (3) to identify the various Marxist groups whose research is to be evaluated.

In Chapter 2, the research-relevant epistemological perspectives of the different Marxist groups are examined systematically and compared with those required by the generally accepted model of contemporary social science inquiry and the policymaking model outlined in Chapter 1. The discussion covers theories of knowledge, views of determinism, fatalism, voluntarism, the relationship of the whole to its parts, empiricism, positivism, neutrality, and objectivity. Certain positions on these matters tend to go together, to require consistency with one another, and to jointly influence views of method, science, and research. We will see that a materialist epistemological perspective is essential to the generally accepted model of research. Other epistemological assumptions, idealist in character, either rule out the need for research or enjoin any possibility of undertaking it along the lines required by the generally accepted model. Some Marxist orientations share the materialist epistemological views required for competent, defensible social science; others hold epistemological views radically incompatible with them.

In Chapter 3, the central methodological assumptions required in any mode of inquiry are examined as they appear in contemporary Marxism. They include the character of the research process (inductive versus deductive, beginning with the concrete or the abstract), the importance of observation and interpretation, the meaning of data, the nature of concepts and indicators, the form of explanation (dialectical or causal), and the construction, testing, and application of theory. These methodological options are influenced by the epistemological orientations outlined in Chapter 2. Certain methodological choices will be shown to promote research recognized as valuable in terms of the generally accepted model; others make inquiry nearly impossible. It will also be shown that in the absence of specific methodological choices, research cannot provide the empirical basis for intervention and action.

In Chapter 4, Marxist views of modern science are explored, how Marxists see their own research with respect to science is described, and how they understand the relationship of science to class and to politics is explained. In each case emphasis is on the implications of these matters for research quality. Certain perspectives on these points encourage research that is defensible by reference to contemporary social science and useful for policymaking; others do not.

In short, in Chapters 2 through 4 it will be shown that some Marxists hold epistemological views that are actually hostile to research. They tend to reject the methodological options required for carrying it out in an acceptable way. Their understanding of science is incompatible with valid inquiry. Those whose epistemological assumptions are consistent with the requirements of contemporary social science are quite likely to hold methodological principles and a view of science that are equally acceptable to non-Marxists.

Chapter 5 considers how Marxists actually undertake inquiry in terms of the research strategies and the research techniques they employ and how this is influenced by their assumptions about inquiry. All types of contemporary Marxists undertake research defined broadly, but they do not agree among themselves about how it should be done. Different assumptions about epistemology, method, and science lead to different conceptions of research and different ways of carrying it out.

In Chapter 6, an overall assessment of the value of Marxist inquiry is made. Marxists are evaluated as to whether or not they use the results of their research to support their knowledge claims and whether or not the research they produce can contribute to solving real world problems. Some Marxists see research as a form of evidence that may sustain knowledge claims. Others do not make this connection. Some Marxists produce research of use in constructing empirical instruments that can be linked to normative structures of choice (systematic considerations of values and preferences) to yield reasoned policy and promote effective intervention and real world action. Others do not have the tools to do this.

## EPISTEMOLOGY, METHOD, AND SCIENCE: A GENERALLY ACCEPTED VIEW OF THE FOUNDATIONS OF KNOWLEDGE

Because Marxist research cannot be described or evaluated in absolute terms, a basis of assessment is needed. For that purpose the generally accepted criteria of inquiry, particularly those relating to epistemology, methodology, and science current in the social sciences, are most appropriate. Throughout this book, allusion to these criteria for research or to the norms of contemporary social science will be a shorthand way of referring to the set of underlying assumptions that lead to knowledge claims or research findings acceptable within the social science community. Points of agreement and disagreement between specific Marxist groups concerning elements of this model will serve as a focus for evaluation.

Although this model is referred to as generally accepted, it is not universally recognized as valid, for much controversy and discussion exist about many of these matters, among non-Marxists as well as Marxists. Neither can it be assumed that all non-Marxists will be satisfied with Marxist research, even if it does fulfill the requirements of contemporary social science, because not all non-Marxists recognize these assumptions. Research, even if it is considered to be satisfactorily grounded by those who carry it out, will not satisfy those who have a different set of assumptions. However, using the generally accepted model of research as a tool here supposes that the preponderance of non-Marxist social scientists would agree with most of its elements.

The norms of contemporary social science are sufficient for our purposes with one exception related to policymaking. In addition to the requirements of the generally accepted model, Marxist research will be assessed, and the resulting knowledge claims made by Marxists will be evaluated in terms of the potential they offer for action or application. Requirements related to this feature of research will be referred to as the policymaking model. Reasoned policy as defined here is a "set of theories able to link specific human actions to a preferred outcome" (Meehan, 1985). Concretely, policies combine analytical, corrigible empirical, or scientific structures, which indicate possible future life conditions, with ethical or normative instruments that similarly rank possible choices in a systematic and rigorous manner. The goal of policymaking is to satisfy human needs or improve the human condition. Ultimately, therefore, policies are evaluated on the basis of their consequences, in terms of their use to humankind. Contemporary social science norms do not require that research results be useful for policymaking, but including this element poses little difficulty. Most of the assumptions of the generally accepted model are consistent with it; the policymaking model supplements the generally accepted view. Adding it here facilitates the understanding and use of Marxist research by those non-Marxists involved in decision-making.

Contemporary social science includes a specific, agreed upon core of assumptions, widely viewed as essential to a valid research enterprise. They refer to the foundations of knowledge itself and to how reality is perceived and understood (epistemology), how we study it (method), and how it relates to what is called science. The assumptions about inquiry inherent in the generally accepted model are justifiable in that they tend to go along with the production of research which in the past has proved to be at least potentially useful and corrigible. Of course, this is no guarantee as to the future utility of this model.

Here in Chapter 1 the views central to the generally accepted model are simply presented. In Chapters 2, 3, and 4, they will be compared with assumptions made by the various Marxist groups.

We will begin with what have come to be common epistemological assumptions underlying research. Contemporary social science leans toward materialism rather than idealism. This influences its understanding of a theory of knowledge, determinism, fatalism, voluntarism, the relationship between the whole and its parts, empiricism, positivism, neutrality, and objectivity.

By opting for a materialist rather than an idealist theory of knowledge, contemporary social science assumes that knowledge is indispensably intersubjective (in the sense that it is accessible to two or more subjects, that is, objective), that it reflects a real world that exists independently of the researcher, and that it is collected under a specific scientific practice with socially established rules of observation, reporting, replication, and so forth. The generally accepted model rejects a theory of knowledge that contends that the world exists only in the mind of the researcher and that scientific knowledge is merely a personal construction or creation.

Some measure of determinism is another epistemological prerequisite to successful inquiry. Neither the view that human behavior is completely the result of free will (voluntarism) nor the fatalistic belief that human behavior is entirely decided by factors outside the control of individual humans can be maintained. In its more acceptable form, determinism assumes that human action is consistent rather than random, at the same time leaving room for human intervention. This makes it possible to attribute responsibility for certain actions to specific individuals.

The generally accepted model of research is based on the assumption that the whole and its parts are interrelated. Without assuming that the parts (e.g., individual behavior, institutions, or analytical sudivisions of society) can be mechanically added up to constitute the whole (e.g., society), modern social science research assumes that information about the parts is relevant for understanding or dealing with the whole. The view that the whole unilaterally determines the character of the parts is rejected.

As defined by these contemporary norms, research is more likely to succeed when it is directed by assumptions that include empiricism. This does not, however, require accepting either blind, crude empiricism or classical empiricism (which defines experience in a subjectivist and an idealist manner). The generally accepted model is also positivist in certain respects, for it assumes the methodological unity of natural and social science, the testability of knowledge, and a qualitative difference in objective and value judgments. This form of positivism does not necessitate accepting Comte's "positive philosophy" or all the tenets of modern logical positivism.

Serious research requires an effort to be objective with respect to what is being studied, but it does not demand that research be "value-free" or that those undertaking research be neutral in the sense of not caring about the subject matter under investigation. It does assume that the researcher can separate the self from what is being studied, though it is probably impossible to eliminate all distortion or prejudice. Social scientists are not condemned to total, complete subjectivity and relativism just because they are human and the object of their study is the social realm.

The generally accepted model of research also includes a set of methodological principles and procedures considered essential to the production of defensible research. They pertain to the research process itself (deduction versus induction; a concrete versus an abstract point of departure), the character of observation and interpretation, the meaning of data and concepts, the explanatory forms for expressing the rules that constitute theory (e.g., causal, dialectical, teleological), and the methodological requirements of theory (construction, testing, and application). The methodological assumptions of contemporary social science require a certain empirical grounding in evidence with respect to all these dimensions.

Research entails both deductive and inductive activities. It is inductive when it generalizes from observations. It is deductive when it examines the implications of specific theories, applying the general principle to specific cases. A *priori* deduction which consists of postulating a formal set of relationships and examining their logical consequences is not acceptable if such activity is set apart from all reference to testing by observation and comparison with evidence or if it is organized so that it automatically passes every possible test as a result of internal self-definition.

Contemporary social research assumes that astute observation permits one to produce knowledge that goes beyond appearances, beyond the self-evident, to get at underlying causes. In the process of observation, one identifies and selects from the complexity of the real world that which is interesting for the particular purposes of a study and omits that which is irrelevant.

Interpretation is part of the set of procedures associated with research. In terms of the general model, it is not a process of creating a reality but rather one of discovery, valid only when constrained by reference to evidence. There may be any number of non-conflicting interpretations of what is being observed. But these should not be contradictory or inconsistent with each other.

The meaning of data and their role in research are central to a generally accepted model of research. Data are defined here as descriptions, symbolic statements, about reality produced by observation and interpretation. Data constitute the most basic level of processed information resulting from the observation of the incoming flow of raw perceptions of the real world. Data are assumed to reflect reality and to be of use in understanding it, rather than constructed or invented in the sense of being arbitrary.

Concepts are tools for identifying, organizing, and setting the bounds of what is observed. It is preferable that concepts be defined in real terms rather than nominal terms and that they be linked to indicators that permit measured values to be assigned to the variables that represent them.

Explanatory forms and theories are also integral elements of the generally accepted model. Explanatory forms refer to the patterns of relationships among data observed in the world around us. Theories are composed of rule-like statements of regularities expressed in terms of these explanatory forms. Causality is an example. Theories consist of these types of generalizations that can be tested and that guide inquiry. The policymaking model adds to this definition of theory the requirement that explanatory forms be causal in character so that they can serve as the basis for intervention. The methodological dimensions of theory concern its construction, testing, and application. A theory must be constructed with reference to observation and data, and its concepts must be defined in real terms. It should be tested against reality with reference to evidence. Evidence takes on a variety of forms. Application is central to justifying theory within the terms of the policymaking model.

Specific assumptions about *science* underlie modern social science. Science refers to the whole process of doing research and producing knowledge systematically and rigorously. Based on observation, it seeks to organize and explain, directly or indirectly, the data that constitute the basic material of research. Its general method is to isolate elements and specify relationships. Its final goal is the synthesis of these elements and processes. Science is assumed to be of general utility for humankind. This notion is central to the policymaking model as well. None of this denies that science can be manipulated and distorted, that is, used for the ends of one group rather than those of another. But ultimately science is assumed to have a neutral core. It is not class determined. Politics should not be put above science in the sense of dictating, in advance, either methods or research results. Science should be independent of any particular political ideology.

The generally accepted model of research employed here for purposes of evaluating the various Marxist views is presented in a relatively strict form. This sets a very demanding requirement for Marxist research. Such an approach is not without merit, for if Marxist research is to be of use to non-Marxists it must meet recognized standards. At the same time this model is admittedly idealized and stereotyped, presenting a view of inquiry that does not always conform to reality despite the best intentions of those involved in research.

## CONTEMPORARY MARXIST ORIENTATIONS

The discussion in this book is organized around four Marxist orientations: the philosophic Marxists, the materialist Marxists, the structuralist Marxists, and the deductivist Marxists. These categories are not exhaustive. Other Marxist groups, such as the realist Marxists, could have been included had space and time permitted. These same Marxists could have been classified according to different criteria. *But the value of these categories is that they group together individuals (1) who share certain assumptions about epistemology, method, and science which influence how they approach research, (2) who have adopted the same general research strategies and techniques, and (3) whose research results can be used as evidence for defending knowledge claims and as a basis for producing policy.* Exceptions, notably with respect to the structuralists on these points, will be indicated as we proceed.

The use of any system of classification has advantages and disadvantages. Dividing Marxists into the categories used here is useful given the goal of making Marxist research accessible to non-Marxists because, taken together, they cover the whole spectrum, from Marxists whose research is likely to be of great interest, to those whose research is virtually useless. But caution is warranted. Any system of categories can overlook or ignore important differences between members of a group. Certain individuals assigned to a particular Marxist category do not share all the views attributed to that group. Human thought and action are too complicated to expect absolute conformity or consistency. Classifying any particular individual as belonging to one particular Marxist orientation rather than another is also difficult because people evolve and change over the years; Theodor Adorno is an example. In addition, at certain points in time and in some countries (for example, Stalinist USSR) for reasons of professional and personal survival Marxists in certain groups have had to disguise their real views or even feign acceptance of an opposing Marxist perspective with which they disagreed. Finally, the views of a few Marxists such as A. Gramsci or L. Goldmann are so complex as to make it almost impossible to categorize them. Despite the oversimplification and the exceptions involved, the value of these categories still outweighs the disadvantages if they assist non-Marxists in understanding Marxist research.

In introducing these Marxist orientations, we will identify their precursors within the Marxist tradition, indicate some individuals and groups who can be classified as members of each current, locate them in terms of history and country of residence, and establish their general policymaking experience. The last-named is potentially significant because it may influence how they construct and test theory, and whether or not they think it important to apply their research findings to real world problems.

The first group, the philosophic Marxists, also referred to here as simply the philosophics, represents the romantic dimension of Marxism. They are closely linked to the tradition of philosophical idealism. The group includes the phenomenologically oriented Marxists like Paul Piccone and Enzo Paci, the Neo-Hegelians Georg Lukacs and Karl Korsch and their successors such as Agnes Heller, Freudians such as Wilhelm Reich and Herbert Marcuse, existentialists such as Jean-Paul Sartre and Maurice Merleau-Ponty, some of the Trotskyists, most of the Yugoslavian Praxis group, the critical theorists such as Jürgen Habermas, (until very recently) and most of the post–1930 Frankfurt school (Theodor Adorno after 1956). The philosophic Marxists have dominated Western Marxism since the 1920s. They have seldom held power, however, and they have generally refused to participate in parliamentary politics.

A second major stream within Marxism includes the pragmatic, practical, even anti-idealist, anti-philosophic Marxists who will here be labelled materialist Marxists or simply materialists. Precursors of this orientation include the pre–1930 Frankfurt school (Carl Grunberg), the Austro-Marxists (especially Rudolf Hilferding, Karl Renner, and Otto Bauer but not Max Adler), the Marxists of the Second International such as Karl Kautsky and Edward Bernstein, and the various official Communist parties and Marxist-Leninist formations that emerged during specific historical periods. Georgy Plekhanov and Nikolai Bukharin were leading historical figures of this orientation. Important contemporary materialists include individuals as diverse as Thomas Bottomore, Sebastiano Timpanero, and Ralph Miliband in the West and B. Kedrov or G. Osipov (in the 1960s) in the USSR and Stanislav Ossowski, Jan Szczepanski, and Radovan Richta in Eastern Europe. The materialists have been in and out of power in the socialist countries and in certain Western countries as well (as a result of their participation in parliamentary-oriented Communist Party formations). They exercised authority in the USSR during the 1920s and again under Nikita Khrushchev between the mid–1950s and the late 1960s. They appear to be regaining influence with the arrival of Mikhail Gorbachev in office. The materialists have held control of government and polity in

China from time to time in the post-revolutionary period. Since Mao's death the materialists appear to be in power.

The third group, the structuralist Marxists, represents a recent development in the last thirty years. It originated in France where it was most influential from the early 1960s through the early 1980s. It is still important in the United States and Great Britain. The primary characteristic of this group is a commitment to understanding society in terms of structures. They reject either an essentially idealist or an exclusively materialist view of the world and seek instead to reconcile the two by integrating what they consider to be the most interesting aspects of each. They are influenced by various non-Marxist structuralists in the fields of psychology, anthropology, and linguistics including Jean Piaget, Claude Levi-Strauss, Ferdinand de Saussure, and Gaston Bachelard. Louis Althusser has contributed far more than anyone else to the development of structuralist Marxism. Other important structuralists who at one time or another were considered to be Marxists include Jacques Lacan, Maurice Godelier, Göran Therborn, Manuel Castells, Nicos Poulantzas, Michel Foucault, and David Harvey. The influence of this form of Marxism has been largely limited to the intellectual community.

The fourth group, the deductivist Marxists, or simply the deductivists, is Stalinist in political orientation and has been concentrated in the socialist countries or the parallel Communist Party formations in the West. They have alternated with the materialists in governing the socialist countries. The deductivists held power and determined research strategy in the USSR during most of the period when Stalin ruled (end of the 1920s until the early 1950s). They returned to power in more moderate guise after the departure of Khrushchev, consolidating their influence in the 1970s and early 1980s. In China the deductivists were in control after the Hundred Flowers Campaign, just prior to and during the Great Leap Forward (1958–62) and during the Cultural Revolution (1966–69).

The deductivists are characterized by a strong insistence that social analysis must follow logically from what Marx, Engels, and Lenin wrote. They have a definite preference for intellectual procedures of a deductive character. The Deborinists were early deductivists in the USSR in the 1920s and 1930s. B. Ukraintsev, M. N. Rutkevich, and N. N. Semenov are important Soviet deductivists today.

All of these Marxist orientations except the structuralist offer a complex combination of ideas about epistemology, method, science, and research which tend to go together in a more or less systematic manner. At the same time, each of the three strongly opposes and criticizes the views on these matters advanced by Marxists in other orientations. The structuralists, on the other hand, show internal agreement on most matters but divide into two groups over how to actually go about research.

# 2.

# MARXISTS ON THE EPISTEMOLOGICAL ASSUMPTIONS OF RESEARCH

An identifiable set of epistemological commitments underlies contemporary social science research; they are often taken for granted and not articulated, but they are broadly agreed upon. These assumptions correspond more closely to philosophical materialism than to idealism. They tend to determine how method is understood, how research is defined and carried out, and how knowledge claims are defended. Research is accepted or rejected by others, at least partly by reference to the epistemological assumptions upon which it is based.

In this chapter the research-relevant epistemological assumptions of the various Marxists groups will be examined and compared with those assumed in contemporary social science. The reader will recall that the generally accepted model of research includes a commitment to philosophical materialism, to a materialist theory of knowledge, to determinism rather than voluntarism or fatalism, to the possibility of learning about the whole from an analysis of its parts, to general empiricism, to objectivity, and to certain aspects of positivism.

The epistemological assumptions of the materialist Marxists (Table 1) are closest to those of the generally accepted model, and their views are influenced mainly by their commitment to philosophical materialism. We will see that they possess a materialist theory of knowledge. They are determinists in a sense required by materialism, and they favor a materialist form of inquiry, that is, analysis that assumes one can learn about the whole by examining

**Table 1**
**Marxist Epistemological Assumptions: Summary Statement for Chapter 2**

| Views on | Materialists | Structuralists | Philosophics | Deductivists |
|---|---|---|---|---|
| Theories of Knowledge | Correspondence or reflective Materialist | Mixed | Knowledge constructed by the mind Idealist | Mixed |
| Determinism, Fatalism, Voluntarism | Determinist Anti-fatalist Anti-voluntarist | Anti-voluntarist Structural determinism | Anti-determinist Voluntarism ok | Fatalist and voluntarist |
| Whole Versus the Parts | No priority to the totality Elements are important | Interaction of totality and parts | Totality all important | Totality most important |
| Empiricism: General, Crude, or Classical | General empiricism ok Anti-classical empiricism | Oppose empiricism in any form | Oppose crude and general empiricism Some favor classical empiricism | Oppose all forms of empiricism |
| Positivism | Sympathetic to many elements of positivism | Accept some elements of positivism | Reject positivism | Reject positivism |
| Objectivity | Objectivity is possible | Self-attributed objectivity | Objectivity is impossible or it is linked with a class perspective | Only Marxism-Leninism can be objective |

its elements. Their materialism orients them toward general empiricism and certain aspects of positivism. It leads them to accept objectivity as a legitimate, though not absolute, goal.

Among Marxists, the philosophics are in sharpest disagreement with the epistemological assumptions of contemporary social science. The philosophics' views are close to those of philosophical idealism, which strongly affects their theory of knowledge. Their idealism requires them to reject determinism, it compels them to emphasize the importance of the amorphous totality over its elements, and it obliges them to reject empiricism in those forms compatible with the generally accepted model of research. Idealism requires that they react with hostility toward all aspects of positivism and all efforts at objectivity. These views are apparent in Georg Lukacs's *History and Class Consciousness* (1971), a work that has had an important influence on the philosophics over the years.

The epistemological views of the deductivists and structuralist Marxists lie midway between the two extremes of idealism and materialism. As formulated by Louis Althusser the epistemological assumptions of the structuralists combine what is claimed to be the best elements of both fundamental epistemological positions. The result is a clever, though sometimes contradictory, theory of knowledge fused with a qualified commitment to what Althusser calls "determinism" and "objectivity," and a view of the totality and parts as interacting. The idealist aspects of their views require them to reject empiricism. The materialist dimension of their thought demands that they accept certain components of positivism. The structuralists agree with some of the epistemological norms that have come to be associated with contemporary social science research but reject others. Althusser's *For Marx* and his *Reading Capital*, co-authored with E. Balibar, are principal sources of inspiration for the structuralists.

The deductivists' epistemological views are, as is the case with the structuralists, a mixture of idealism and materialism. But because the deductivists have produced less formal writing about their epistemological opinions than the other Marxist orientations considered here, it is difficult to adequately outline their views. They appear to vacillate between an extreme form of determinism called fatalism and absolute voluntarism. They reject empiricism and positivism; the totality is all important for them. They define a Marxist-

Leninist point of view as objective on an ad hoc basis. Their views are best summarized in the various writings published under Stalin's name.

## IDEALISM, MATERIALISM, AND A THEORY OF KNOWLEDGE

Epistemological assumptions about reality underlie all research. They are materialist, idealist, or a combination of elements of both. In the case of most Marxists, epistemological assumptions relating to inquiry are logically interrelated with each other to form a consistent view of the foundations of knowledge, how it is perceived and comprehended.

The generally accepted view of epistemology required by contemporary social science is materialist rather than idealist. It assumes a reflective or correspondence theory of knowledge rather than a view of knowledge as constructed-by-the-mind. This is because *materialism and a materialist view of knowledge assume a common reality outside of individual mental processes, to be studied, reported, communicated to others, and acted upon. Idealism and an idealist theory of knowledge deny this to be the case.*

Marxists are deeply split over idealism and materialism and over the theories of knowledge and other epistemological assumptions related to each. In general, the philosophics are closer to idealism and the materialists to materialism. The structuralists construct an innovative combination of what they see as the best elements of materialism and idealism. The deductivists' position is also a selective mixture of the two points of view. It is not always easy to identify the views of a particular Marxist group on these matters. Thorough criticisms have been made of both extreme materialism and exaggerated idealism, and in order to escape judgment many Marxists qualify their views substantially or purposely state their positions ambiguously.

While influenced by idealism and materialism, Marxist views on the whole collection of questions related to epistemology may or may not result in an overall coherent set of epistemological assumptions about research. The philosophic Marxists' epistemological assumptions, while internally consistent, are incompatible with the generally accepted model of social science. The assumptions of the materialists are also internally consistent but are more in line with those of contemporary social science. The views of the deductivists and the structuralists are internally inconsistent, constructed of a combination of assumptions, some of which are shared by contemporary social science and some of which are incompatible with it.

The terms "materialism," "idealism," and "theory of knowledge" are used here in the sense in which they are generally recognized. Materialism is defined as according priority to material reality and to the concrete rather than to thought. Being is assumed to precede consciousness, although this does not require one to deny the significance of thought itself. The world around us is assumed to exist independently of people and their minds, but humans may modify nature and mold their environment. Idealism, on the other hand, is understood to maintain that the existence of the world and of nature, independently of people, is dubious. In the extreme it holds that reality is in some way mental, a mere construction of the mind, knowable only through consciousness, with no meaning beyond it. Thought is prior to existence. Idealism and materialism are pertinent for understanding Marxist research because each is linked to a different theory of knowledge. A theory of knowledge pertains to the relation of human perception to reality. Can we understand what is really happening in the world? Does that world actually exist or is it rather a construction of the mind?

Theories of knowledge are essentially either materialist or idealist. The materialists and the philosophics have opposite theories of knowledge. Their differences parallel those of idealism and materialism closely. The other Marxists combine elements from both into their theories of knowledge.

## A Correspondence or Reflective Theory of Knowledge: The Materialist Marxists

Most materialist Marxists have a correspondence or reflective theory of knowledge similar to that required by contemporary social science. A correspondence theory, materialist in character, holds that what one perceives, senses, and observes corresponds to reality. Thought provides an exact image of what exists. This is an unrealistic view of the world in the sense that perception is never wholly accurate or absolutely complete. The reflective theory of knowledge is more sophisticated. It holds that people acquire information from what they see and experience. Although this knowledge is not a photographic reproduction of the world itself, it is a reflection of what is going on. Both the correspondence and reflective theories of knowledge are treated together here because both are materialist. Both insist on the autonomous, objective character of the world, arguing that ultimately there is only one reality, though this reality may be contradictory and complex. Both of these theories of knowledge reject the idealist claim that what each person sees and experiences is necessarily different from what others see and experience.

The reflective theory of knowledge grants that reality may be open to different perceptions without this inevitably leading to relativism or subjectivism. It does not deny that perception may be inaccurate for a number of reasons. It allows for the possibility that many things we cannot even see or perceive, unobservables, really exist and can be studied by means of indirect measurement.

### Knowledge as Constructed by the Mind: The Philosophic Marxists

The philosophic Marxists tend toward idealism and reject those theories of knowledge associated with the generally accepted model of research. They refer to the correspondence theory of knowledge derogatorily as the "mirror theory of knowledge." They are equally critical of the reflective theory of knowledge. Skeptical about people's ability to seize knowledge directly and immediately from either experience or systematic study, they argue for an idealist, sometimes Hegelian, theory of knowledge. Almost all the philosophics say that knowledge is constructed or created actively by the mind. Reality does not exist independently of knowledge about it. Consciousness and thought are products of the intellect, which exists apart from the world. In the extreme this means the external world is merely an artifact of consciousness. It does not really exist but is only a mental construction.

## The Structuralists' Theory of Knowledge

The structuralists' theory of knowledge falls between that of absolute correspondence or reflection and that of absolute mental construction. It is difficult to locate their theory as either clearly idealist or distinctly materialist. They bring together an imaginative combination of epistemological assumptions that include elements from both idealism and materialism. Althusser maintains that ultimately the superiority of one over the other cannot be proved (Althusser, 1971:57–58). The structuralists see reality as a system of internal relations or structures, which cannot be viewed at all—either directly or indirectly. These structures, which are continually fusing, dividing, and recombining, constitute society or social formations. Reality is hidden beneath the surface, disguised. Appearances are deceptive. There is no possibility of linking observable evidence to these underlying structures. For some structuralists these problems are serious enough to require that they reject a materialist theory of knowledge and opt for idealism. They argue that all we know about the world and its structures is produced in thought alone. Reality is accessible only to the mind. Althusser suggests that the object of knowledge, the object-in-thought, is absolutely distinct from the real object, the external concrete thing-in-itself. Thought and reality are entirely separate realms. At the same time, the structuralists' view of the world is materialist, in that they argue that there is only one objective structural reality, though it may be in constant flux.

## The Deductivists' Theory of Knowledge

The deductivists' theory of knowledge, like that of the structuralists, is a blend. It is idealist to the extent that it gives priority to theory (in the form of historical materialism) over evidence and materialist in that it offers a non-metaphysical reading of reality. Stalin, an important deductivist, seemingly supported the idealist view that the mind, or consciousness, plays the most important role in the process of cognition (Graham, 1972:366). But at other points he defended an extreme materialist theory of knowledge, a correspondence view, contending that thought and the mind were composed of matter and could be fully understood as such.

### Theories of Knowledge and Defensible Research

The materialist Marxists' theory of knowledge is the same as that required to undertake research in terms accepted by contemporary social science. That of the philosophics conflicts with the generally accepted view. This means that the materialists are more likely than the philosophics to produce knowledge that is legitimate within the terms of contemporary social science. Both the structuralist and deductivist Marxists have theories of knowledge and views of materialism and idealism that are ambiguous, neither entirely materialist nor authentically idealist. Their understanding of these matters does not, by itself, preclude research of interest and value to non-Marxists. Their position on other epistemological and methodological questions must be examined before a more definite assessment can be made.

## DETERMINISM, FATALISM, AND VOLUNTARISM

Contemporary social science assumes determinism in its efforts to describe human behavior. If there were no regularity in the social world, research designed to uncover causal relations and predict the consequences of action would be a fruitless waste of time. The major epistemological alternatives to determinism are voluntarism and fatalism, both of which are incompatible with contemporary social science research. Fatalism assumes everything is predetermined by unknowable forces, voluntarism that nothing can be predicted because human behavior is exclusively the result of conscious reflection. An examination of the various Marxists' positions on these questions reveals that the philosophics opt for voluntarism, the deductivists for a combination of voluntarism and fatalism, the materialists for determinism, and the structuralists for a special form of structural determinism.

### Determinism

Determinism holds that all phenomena, and human intervention itself, are logical and lawful rather than chaotic, haphazard, arbitrary, or random. Events are seen to be interconnected in a systematic manner rather than isolated and senseless. Determinism affirms that events are predictable, that they follow definite patterns of regularity if certain specific conditions are met. People do not function on the basis of free will alone. They are constrained by external conditions. *Defensible research in terms of contemporary social science assumes this kind of determinism.*

Most materialist Marxists are determinists (Rossman, 1981:145). They maintain that everything that happens is caused by specific factors that can be studied and understood. In general, objective conditions are held to affect existence and restrain human action. For some, this is manifest through economic determinism. Material life conditions are said to influence mental states, "consciousness, will and conduct rather than vice versa." Whatever the form, these materialist Marxists regard society as lawful in the sense that "inherent objective regularity characterizes it" (Mshvenieradze and Osipov, 1966).

None of the other Marxists accepts determinism as clearly as do the materialists. The philosophics are strongly opposed to determinism. The potential for human action on the basis of choice, of free will, is central to their understanding of the world. They see determinism as mechanical, as denying people's humanity. The structuralist Marxists give priority to structures rather than to individuals in opting for determinism. They reject a rigid form of economic determinism at the structural level, but they do advocate structural determinism. The deductivists are inconsistent, wavering between an absolute rejection of determinism and the acceptance of it in an extreme form known as fatalism.

### Fatalism

Fatalism holds that everything is prearranged or predetermined. The future is fixed in advance by a "fate" or *fatum*. Things are determined beforehand, by forces that are beyond the powers of human beings to understand or to influence. From the individual's point of view everything appears to be unpredictable. Events just happen, with no apparent specific connection to anything else. They are unknowable as well as inescapable (Bunge, 1959:101). *A fatalist view of the world makes research in terms of the generally accepted model unnecessary, perhaps even impossible.*

Fatalism is associated with the writings of many of the deductivists and follows from their extreme economism, that is, their exaggeration of the significance of economic factors relative to other variables. Stalin and the deductivists, for example, argue that developments in the social, cultural, and intellectual spheres arise inevitably and independently from the economic base. Certain laws govern society with such force that change through human intervention is impossible (Stalin, 1972). Althusser and the structuralists strive to avoid this form of economic determinism leading to fatalism by arguing that overdetermination assures that the economy dominates the other structures only in specific historical situations and then only in the last instance. This provides a rather large degree of autonomy for non-economic structures. The philosophics are not fatalists, though those among this group who emphasize the influence of an unknowable, outside force, share a point with fatalism. The materialists reject fatalism completely (Bukharin, 1925:51).

### Voluntarism

Voluntarism goes to the other extreme and assumes that human agency, free will, is the principal force for explaining any particular outcome or event in the world. Extreme voluntarists imply that one can will a situation into existence, that change can be initiated by will power alone, no matter what obstacles or impediments are present. *The voluntarists' view of the world is hostile to social science research because it assumes that human behavior is the result of unpredictable conscious human reflection wholly independent of specific definable causal factors.*

Most of the philosophics are voluntarists. They assume an "intentional, teleological character of [human] action" (Bleicher, 1980:257). This is consistent with their idealist theory of knowledge which gives primacy to consciousness, to ideas, to the spirit, and to free will. They believe human nature is intrinsically creative and flexible. "All men and women are potentially active agents in the construction of their social world and their personal lives" (Comstock, 1980:1). If they do not realize this potential, as Herbert Marcuse argues, it is because they are ideologically manipulated by capitalism, bureaucracy, consumerism, advanced technology, and so on. The philosophics doubt that people's behavior is predictable or determined. On the contrary, they view it as spontaneous, based on consciousness, free of external influence or constraint. History can be the freely chosen project of individuals. People are potentially self-consciously creating their own world in a process of imaginative self-realization.

The structuralists are opposed to voluntarism, tending to minimize the individual's influence on social formations. Human will has no place in their analysis. Their rejection of the subject (person) in history and their emphasis on structural factors and process make for a denial of voluntarism's human agency.

The materialists see voluntarism in its extreme form as mere sentimentalism. More generally, it is considered inconsistent with their commitment to determinism, for they understand it to require an idealist view of the world which they reject.

The deductivists are not voluntarists in the same sense as the philosophics, and yet some aspects of their thought are close to this view, especially on those topics concerning science and research. Many deductivists in the state socialist countries assume that reality can be made to conform to the political line of the Communist Party (Szczepanski, 1966:47). They presume that the Party can mold reality to its view regardless of objective circumstances. When the deductivists were in power, the Communist Party regularly set goals in an almost arbitrary manner, with little attention to concrete circumstances or aspects of society that were inconsistent with their theories (Joravsky, 1961:203–20; Lewin, 1974:202; Kolakowski, 1978c:77). This implies confidence in the power of will as opposed to determinism, a belief that change can be imposed voluntaristically, from above, by the Party. Of course, this position contradicts the fatalist aspects of the deductivists' epistemological views discussed earlier, but they seem less concerned with internal consistency than with the maintenance of dogma.

### Research Implications of Determinism, Fatalism, and Voluntarism

As a result of the philosophics' voluntarism and the absolute priority they assign to free human action, they fail to distinguish between fatalism and determinism and consequently reject both. They are led to deny the possibility of social science research which assumes phenomena are lawful. If human behavior is not regular in

some ways, there is little hope of generalizing about it from systematic inquiry. If people's behavior is not lawful, but rather exclusively the result of unpredictable conscious choice, if individuals
can go beyond their past and present experience at any moment
as the philosophics contend, then humans cannot be studied using
the generally accepted criteria of research. If people do as they
choose, without being influenced by outside factors in a regular
and consistent manner, research is limited to momentary description and anecdote. Prediction and generalization are excluded; intervention with known results is impossible.

The fatalism of the deductivists is also inconsistent with contemporary social science which requires study and validation in experience rather than basing knowledge on arbitrary presuppositions.
Fatalism assumes an overriding *fatum*. Its mechanical predeter-
mination removes the necessity for objective study of the human
situation in all its complexity as a prerequisite of understanding
and predictable action. Fatalists don't undertake inquiry but rather
make sets of assumptions about reality and deduce from them a
series of resultant expectations. This procedure rules out any need
for research. Inquiry would be impossible in any case because the
*fatum* who determines all is assumed to be beyond the influence
of normal human beings.

Only determinism, as a position, is compatible with the belief
that phenomena can be studied and understood within the terms
of contemporary social science. Among the Marxists, the materialists support determinism and the structuralists advocate a form
of structural determinism. These views are consistent with the generally accepted model concerning how to carry out research and
produce findings. The voluntarism of the philosophics and the deductivists' dual fatalist-voluntarist views militate against their producing valid findings except accidentally.

## THE RELATIONSHIP BETWEEN THE WHOLE AND ITS
PARTS: THE QUESTION OF THE TOTALITY

The relation of the parts to the whole is not an epistemological
question of central concern to contemporary social science. There
is broad agreement that one analyzes or systematically studies the
parts or elements in order to come to a better understanding of

the whole no matter how complex that totality may be. The importance of analysis, defined as the breaking down of complex structures or complex processes into constituent elements, is taken for granted. In short, the generally accepted model rejects the view that the totality is all important or that it has mystical qualities that cannot be revealed by studying its constituent elements.

The relation of the parts to the whole is a topic of controversy among Marxists. They cannot even agree on which of two words, the "whole" or the "totality," is most appropriate for referring to the largest unit of inquiry. In this section we will see that the materialist Marxists share the generally accepted view of modern social science concerning the relationship between the whole and its parts. The philosophics and the deductivists hold that the totality is all important, that it is inseparable from its constituent elements, and that it determines the parts. The structuralists hold a compromise view somewhere in between the two extremes.

How Marxists view the relation of the whole to its parts has implications for inquiry, either assisting them or hindering them in their attempts to focus their research, to undertake analysis, and to adopt a research strategy consistent with that of the generally accepted model.

### The Totality Is All Important: The Philosophics and the Deductivists

The philosophics regard society as a dynamic totality in which all the parts or elements are in constant interaction, "interpenetrating." Reciprocal feedback between the parts and the totality occurs immediately. For these Marxists, the totality takes on an idealist, abstract, mystical, metaphysical existence or a spiritual quality. It has priority over the parts, which are viewed as incomplete manifestations of the larger totality.

For the philosophics, the totality is an expression of a single, dominant theme or inner essence that may change through history but is always present and prior. In the recent past the central essence has been capitalism. This theme, they argue, permeates every aspect of the elements of the totality (culture, politics, and so on). The parts cannot be understood by themselves without reference to the totality; the totality can never be understood as the sum of its elements. For the philosophics a non-reductionist analysis must give priority to the totality.

The deductivists' view of the totality is very similar to that of the philosophics. The whole is abstract, metaphysical, an immutable category. The only significant aspect of the parts worthy of study is their relation to the totality (Gorman, 1982:97). Like the philosophics, the deductivists propose that the totality has an essence that molds the various parts of the whole.

### No Special Priority to the Totality: The Materialists and the Structuralists

The materialists are less likely than the philosophics to focus attention on the whole (which is the term they prefer). In any case, it is not the central concept of their analysis. They view it primarily as the object of many influences, a synthesis of distinct elements, each of which can be studied individually (Mshvenieradze and Osipov, 1966:13; McQuarie, 1978:225), though this varies depending on the different degrees of cohesion and inter-dependence of the individual elements (Timpanaro, 1975:193). The materialists reject any definition of it as possessing metaphysical qualities (Bottomore, 1978:74). When they do refer to the whole, they give it a concrete definition. They accord even less importance to the effect of the whole on its parts, attributing no special magical priority to the whole over the parts. To focus on it exclusively contains the risk of being idealist (Timpanaro, 1975:190). The materialists concentrate on one element of the whole, that is, the economic infrastructure, and study its influence on the other parts of the whole.

The structuralists, and especially Althusser, are committed to studying the totality or whole which they define as a structure. However, they reorient the dynamic of the totality in favor of the increased autonomy of the parts relative to the totality. Neither do they deny that the parts tell us something of interest about the totality. Each element in the totality (economic, political, theoretical, and ideological) is influenced by the others, but each has its own rhythm of historical development and its own contradictions or internal problems. The structuralists agree that the parts are a direct manifestation of the totality, but they do not see the parts as necessarily reflecting the dominant theme present in the totality.

The parts cannot be understood without considering their relations with one another and the contribution each makes to the continued existence of the totality (Althusser and Balibar, 1968:100; Althusser, 1965:205–6). In effect, the structuralists seek to have it both ways. They emphasize the influence of the whole on the parts and the effects of the different parts on each other as well. But they are less inclined than the materialists to treat the parts as collectively constituting the whole.

The structuralist Marxists also give a lower priority to the economic element of the whole than do the materialists. The structuralists reject the view that the economic is merely the expression of the other parts; rather, they say it determines which of the parts will ultimately play a dominant role in society at any particular point in time. But like the materialists, the structuralists grant that in the "last instance" the economic wins out over the other parts. Althusser, however, adds a warning to the effect that the "last instance" never arrives.

### Research Implications of the Relationship of the Whole and Its Parts

What are the research implications of the various Marxist views of the totality and its parts? If, as the philosophics and the deductivists contend, the totality is more important than the parts, if the parts are dependent on the totality, if they are in constant interaction with each other and the totality, if the whole is more than the sum of its parts, then research becomes very difficult to focus. This totality is too vast and complex to be studied in its entirety with the research tools currently available. It is impossible to bring evidence to bear on this conception of the totality. The result is an obscurantist holism, unrelated to reality (Lewontin and Levins, 1976:63).

The philosophics and deductivists do not permit isolating elements of the whole, even momentarily, or breaking the whole into its constituent parts for study. They reject the possibility of accumulating information by systematically studying the parts to gain an understanding of the whole. These Marxists seek to grasp the totality directly. For them, scientific inquiry which focuses on the various elements offers at most only partial truth "which simply distracts attention from the whole" (McInnes, 1972:158). For those who accept this view of the relation of the totality and its parts, the generally accepted view of research can play but a limited role in the acquisition of knowledge. The search for an understanding of the "totality" becomes a utopian odyssey of the intellect.

In addition, the philosophics' belief that the totality has an "essence" that "determines" all the parts of the whole is both fatalistic and deductive. It is fatalistic because it assumes that a single theme is all determining, that knowledge of the parts is automatic once the whole is adequately understood. It is deductive because the means by which the theme is discovered depends not on a comparison with reality or on evidence, but comes instead through abstract reasoning from *a priori* assumptions on the part of the researcher.

The structuralist view of the relation of the parts to the whole is more compatible with the generally accepted model of research than the point of view of either the philosophics or the deductivists. This is because they see the parts as semi-autonomous and the whole as at least in part a function of its elements. Structuralists would, however, object to the strategy adopted by contemporary social science: simplifying and analytically separating the parts from the whole in the short term, for greater knowledge of the whole in the long run.

The structuralists' conception of the totality poses an additional problem for research. Because, according to the structuralists, the totality and its elements are structures, research that focuses on the human individual must be rejected. The structuralists look for explanation in the dynamic interconnection of the parts and the whole rather than in the action of individual members of society. This rejection of the human "subject" as an object of valid research prohibits social science inquiry from examining individual human beings as constituent elements of any whole.

The materialists are the only group whose view of the totality permits a research strategy compatible with the generally accepted epistemological view in social science. They maintain that studying the parts of society ultimately contributes to a better understanding of the whole and leads to a situation where intervention for specific goals is possible. One problem with the way some materialists have historically understood the relation of the totality and the parts arises from the tendency for many of them to give priority to the economic element of the totality in an *a priori* manner rather than as a result of evidence.

## EMPIRICISM

In this section the various Marxist views of empiricism are described and compared with the generally accepted model. Modern social science inquiry is empiricist. It takes for granted the epistemological assumptions related to an empiricist approach to research. In order to avoid confusion, the discussion of this topic must begin with a brief detour. The various meanings of the term "empiricism" itself must be distinguished. At least three meanings of the word are found in contemporary philosophy. The premises of these various forms of empiricism differ, and they imply conflicting approaches to the conduct of research. Marxist views of empiricism can be understood more easily if these differences are clear.

The first type of empiricism, which can be labelled *classical empiricism*, gives exclusive priority to sense experience defined as a highly personal form of information. All knowledge is said to be necessarily subjective and individualized because each person can only count on his or her particular impressions which cannot be assumed to be the same as those of any other individual. Classical empiricism is opposed not only to religion, but also to reason, to rigorous organized inquiry, to science, to logic, and to all systematic means of acquiring knowledge. Its own method is basically subjective description and introspective. It requires that knowledge be grounded in experience defined as a sort of personalized, immediate, unique, entirely internal, subjective phenomenon. Knowledge is the result of ideographic description without any claim to being objective or to having been tested.

Although classical empiricism is basically metaphysical or idealist, historically it was a substantial improvement over other views of the world. It moved one step toward science because it was grounded in monism rather than dualism (Lewis, 1955:104–5). Monism assumes that society and nature are part of one world. Classical dualism proposes two worlds, one of nature (physical reality) and the other mental (of the mind, the spirit, God). Classical empiricism is not just a shadow from the past. It is regularly resurrected by individuals, some of whom are Marxists, who agree with its epistemological tenets.

The second form of empiricism, modern empiricism or *general empiricism*, assumes that knowledge is acquired through the systematic study of concrete phenomena using rigorous methods to attain objective information. The modern empiricists insist that theories be tested and rejected if found to be false. This general empiricism can be viewed as implying a materialist theory of knowledge, the opposite of classical empiricism's subjective, idealist view.

General empiricism emphasizes the importance, as does classical empiricism, of experience. But in the context of general empiricism, this term refers to directly or indirectly observable experience. For general empiricism, experience is potentially objective, reflecting a real world, independent of the individual. Conclusions derived from personal experience must be tested by systematic and repeated observation, experiments, and research. General empiricism, unlike classical empiricism, acknowledges that phenomena exist which cannot be seen, viewed, heard, or "experienced" directly. It does not deny that what individuals claim about experience may be false or distorted.

The third form of empiricism is called abstract empiricism, logical empiricism, liberal empiricism, or *crude empiricism*. It holds that a statement is factual and true only if it is "empirically testable." An experimental situation is assumed to be the "best" test. Crude empiricism is the exact opposite of classical empiricism in that it rejects the authenticity and value of all information based solely on personal experience. A simple accumulation of facts is seen as sufficient for the advancement of science. Observation and quantification are advocated for their own sake. Theory is assumed to be secondary to measurement and is often viewed as superficial and unnecessary, or it is understood to be constructed directly from accumulated facts or data.

General empiricism is most compatible with contemporary social sciences, although crude empiricism has not been absent from this model. General empiricism is essential to research because it provides the basis for knowledge by way of observation and the concrete means for testing conclusions.

In this section we will see that the philosophic Marxists are sympathetic to classical empiricism and reject those forms of empiricism essential to research. The structuralists and deductivists unequivocally oppose all forms of empiricism. The materialists are in agreement with general empiricism, which is central to contemporary research.

### Empiricism: The Philosophic Marxists and the Deductivist Marxists

The philosophic Marxists disagree with the epistemological views inherent in both crude and general empiricism. Many of the philosophics personify empiricism, holding "it" responsible for a broad collection of abuses including alienation, the unequal distribution of power (Marcuse, 1967:23–33), the defense of the status quo (Israel, 1971), support for the capitalist system (McLellan, 1975:81), and the general oppression of humanity by science (Horton and Filsoufi, 1977). They claim that empiricism ignores history, is antidialectical and hyperfactual. It is said to treat facts as if they were ends in themselves (Adorno, 1969:132), to relegate theory to a secondary role, and to refuse to consider values, preferences, desires, and wants as objective phenomena. Its supposed value-neutrality makes praxis meaningless, they say. In short, the assumptions underlying general empiricism concerning reality and the requirements of research are rejected and scorned by the philosophics.

Very few philosophics discuss classical empiricism per se, but their affinity to it is clear. The philosophics agree with classical empiricism's emphasis on subjective personal experience, which they interpret as sensitivity to consciousness and insight. They understand it to encourage a return to a methodology based in description and intuition—which is viewed as potentially dialectical. The Marxist, G. Gurvitch, defends this form of empiricism (1953:31). Other philosophic Marxists of this view go on to argue that classical empiricism encourages the development of theoretical concepts from the "living context of revolutionary activity," that it assumes subjective experience is a reliable form of knowledge, that it rejects determinism, prediction, objective analysis, statistics, and science (Bandyopadhyay, 1971; Piccone, 1971:24; Bottomore, 1975). Here is an empiricism compatible with both the humanism of certain of the philosophics and their preoccupation with creative human potential and individual development. The Hegelian heritage of these

Marxists requires that they reject crude and general empiricism, but it encourages them to retain it in its classical form.

The deductivists share the philosophics' antipathy for crude empiricism and for general empiricism, which they associate with modern Western "bourgeois" social science. But lacking the humanist dimension of philosophic Marxism, they generally reject classical empiricism as well.

Because the philosophics and deductivists reject general empiricism, it is unlikely that either would undertake studies of interest within the context of contemporary social science research or establish the validity of their findings to the satisfaction of those who accept its epistemological assumptions. The philosophics' acceptance of classical empiricism does not really modify this judgment, for it does not move them closer to the generally accepted model of research. Classical empiricism, by its subjectivism and its concept of experience as strictly personal, denies altogether the utility and possibility of research defensible in terms of contemporary social science. Systematic testing of research results through experiment or trial in practical contexts is alien to classical empiricism because each person's view of reality is, as they define it, different from every other person's view. No valid grounds can be established for preferring one to another.

### The Structuralist Marxists: Anti-Empiricism

The structuralist Marxists reject empiricism in all its forms. Essentially, their critique of crude empiricism is the same as the philosophics. Ignoring the distinction between crude and general empiricism, they refer to both as "modern empiricism" (Althusser, 1965:14) and discard them. Althusser outlines the idealist basis of classical empiricism and its metaphysical content, and associates this form of empiricism with philosophical subjectivism. He divorces his own form of structuralist Marxism from this type of empiricism as well because it attributes more importance to personal experience, to "the conscious will of individuals, their actions and their private undertakings" than to structural reality (Althusser, 1965:127).

Althusser concludes that no inquiry can improve our understanding of society if it is limited to what we sense, or to what we can study using the empiricist procedures of contemporary social science. The research tools of empiricism emphasize quantifiable observation. The structuralists argue that the quantitative study of human behavior, central to empiricism, is unacceptable because statistics cannot go beyond appearances.

For the structuralists, reality is a series of structures that cannot be directly observed or studied with concrete research methods because structures are not part of empirical reality. Theory, which refers to these structures, must be constructed by researchers only through the use of "scientific" reasoning, as based on logical and intellectual coherence (discussed in Chapter 3). In addition, an empiricist view conceives of knowledge as a "real part of the real object, the real structure of the real object" (Althusser and Balibar, 1968:38). This assumes a correspondence between the object and knowledge about-the-object which the structuralists deny is possible.

Finally, the structuralists argue that empiricism is idealist. They say that because empiricism requires looking at individuals, it encourages humanism and historicism which in turn implies an acceptance of idealism. Idealism, Althusser contends, is the unacceptable consequence of all forms of empiricism (Althusser, 1965:228).

The structuralist critique of empiricism is more severe than that of the philosophics. At one fell swoop it rejects not just classical, general, and crude empiricism, but all inquiry acceptable within the norms of contemporary social science.

Although Althusser and the structuralists are anti-empiricists, many of Althusser's students and followers, Nicos Poulantzas, for example, have produced interesting, concrete, even empirical works. This is in part because Althusser himself has revised his position in his more recent work, admitting, for example, that it might be of some use to examine the object itself (Althusser, 1971:110–12). But there is another factor involved. For although empirical inquiry is philosophically alien to Althusser's structuralism, it is not inherently contradictory to structuralism in general. In Chapter 5 we will see how some structuralist Marxists have come to undertake empirical research of interest to many non-Marxists.

## Materialist Marxists: General Empiricists

Most materialist Marxists are general empiricists, although their critics among the philosophic Marxists sometimes present them as crude empiricists. Most of the materialists do not see any incompatibility between general empiricism and Marxism (Nielsen, 1972:266–67). They agree with the materialist content of general empiricism, the theory of knowledge it implies, and its orientation toward the concrete in the form of observable experience. They are opposed, however, to empiricism in its classical form, with its idealism and its denial of the possibility of defensible research. Many of them are equally opposed to crude empiricism. Their research practice is not restricted to collecting and presenting observed facts that are allowed to "speak for themselves." The epistemological views of the materialist Marxists concerning empiricism are very close to those required by the generally accepted model. (For an example of this, see Szczepanski, 1966.)

### Empiricism: Conclusion

In this section Marxist attitudes toward the three basic modes of empiricism (classic, crude, and general) are compared, with particular attention to acceptance of general empiricism because general empiricism is normally considered essential for valid social research. Empiricism is not the only epistemological assumption for determining the usefulness and validity of the knowledge produced by those who conduct research. We have already examined a number of others. A consideration of the epistemological premises of positivism and objectivity follows. But empiricism involves an extremely important set of prime epistemological assumptions required to do acceptable research. It is significant that materialist Marxism is the only Marxist orientation that accepts general empiricism, the form of empiricism essential for arriving at research findings that will be accepted within the social science community. This chapter also showed that the philosophics make no distinction between crude empiricism and general empiricism, rejecting both. Some of them, however, are attracted to classical empiricism. The deductivists and the structuralists reject all forms of empiricism.

### POSITIVISM

Positivism is often taken to be synonymous with rigorous, systematic research. There is little doubt that contemporary social science is positivist in many respects; it overlaps empiricism to a point where some Marxists make no distinction between the two. But as defined here, they are not the same. In this section we will first locate positivism historically, define its current content, and then compare the various Marxist views of it. One of the most important points emerging from this discussion is that all Marxists agree that at least one of the constituent elements of positivism is inconsistent with Marxist inquiry. But it will be argued here that the aspect of positivism which all the Marxists reject is not essential for the production of valid research in terms of the generally accepted model.

Historically, positivism traces its roots to Francis Bacon, the English empiricists, and the philosophers of the Enlightenment. As with empiricism, its early forms were sometimes both idealist and romantic. But unlike empiricism, these forms of positivism have almost disappeared from modern usage. The word "positivism" was coined by Auguste Comte, and it was closely associated with his quite conservative view of politics. Comte argued that society had already passed through the teleological and metaphysical stages of history. His positivist philosophy marked history's culmination in the third and final stage of science. He proposed that the regime in power at the time he was alive had experienced a similar evolution. Having gone through the first two stages of development and reached the third, it deserved unequivocal popular support. His "positivism" thus became a philosophical defense of the status quo.

Modern positivism refers to epistemological matters related to research rather than to a specific political view of the world. It consists of four main components. First, it stresses the similarity between social and natural science, especially with respect to methodology. Second, it holds that knowledge must be subject to testing with evidence, at least in principle. Third, positivism insists that values (normative statements) and facts (empirical statements) are different in kind. Fourth, it contends that research should be value-free and the person undertaking research should be neutral.

The first three elements of positivism outlined here are accepted epistemological assumptions of the generally accepted model of research as outlined in Chapter 1. Without them research is very difficult. First, only if natural science and social science are similar, as held by the generally accepted model, can human behavior be studied systematically with the same basic method which rests on defensible epistemological assumptions. To reject the unity of natural and social science is to place people in a category separate from nature and to assume that they can be studied only with special, philosophically idealist methods. Second, the generally accepted model requires that knowledge be subject to testing; in the absence of evidence, knowledge claims are unconvincing and the empirical instruments needed for policymaking cannot be produced. Third, contemporary social science is positivist in that a distinction is made in terms of the content of normative and empirical statements, that is, there is a separation, of an exclusively logical character, between facts and values.

The fourth element of positivism concerns the value-free character of inquiry and the absolute neutrality of the researcher. The person undertaking a study is supposed to be neutral, an objective observer; inquiry is to be free of any normative engagement. The aim of social science within this positivist framework is to discover the general laws of human behavior without reference to the normative implications involved in the matter. This fourth point in the positivist repertoire is no longer considered essential to contemporary social science. The extreme positivism of the past has given way to a more realistic view of the whole enterprise.

In this discussion the first and fourth elements of positivism, as outlined above, are given the greatest attention. The second and third points, while discussed, are considered in greater detail in the chapters that follow.

We will see that few Marxists give unequivocal support to all the constituent elements of positivism. Some reject it entirely. The fourth element of positivism concerning neutrality and value-free research is troublesome for all Marxists regardless of their orientation. This is one of the rare points on which there is a consensus among the Marxists concerning the epistemological assumptions of research. They all reject value-free inquiry because they assume that knowledge, however it is arrived at, is laden with value-relevant implications. Marxism demands political commitment, and research cannot escape the requirement. Marxists reject the view that those doing research must be neutral in the sense of being disinterested, not caring about their research results. In part, that is because political involvement and taking sides are central to most Marxists' view of the world and efforts to deal with it. This kind of commitment is incompatible with the strict neutrality of positivism. Marxists are consistent on this point. They also argue that neutrality is impossible for non-Marxists as well, because everyone approaches research with a range of predispositions deriving from their personal life experiences, their political and ideological choices, their education, and so on. Marxists conclude that those who claim to be neutral unavoidably contribute to supporting the status quo. While these non-Marxists may view inaction as an indication of neutrality, Marxists argue that, in reality, this amounts to support for what already exists (Baran, 1969:9–10).

What are the research consequences of the Marxist rejection of positivism's value-free inquiry and the neutrality of the researcher? In fact, if, as is maintained here, contemporary social science no longer takes a strict position on these questions, the effect is not serious. The Marxists' stance on the matter does not mean that their research will automatically be incompatible with the norms of contemporary social science.

In this section the Marxists who agree with those aspects of positivism essential to producing research in terms acceptable to today's social science community will be distinguished from those who do not. In examining the views of the various Marxist groups we find, first, that the materialists are qualified positivists. They agree with those aspects of positivism essential to contemporary social science. Second, the structuralists are in partial agreement with positivism, but they still have many objections to it. Third, both the philosophics and deductivists reject positivism entirely, including those of its elements requisite for defensible research.

### The Anti-Positivists: The Philosophics and the Deductivists

The most complete, thoroughgoing denunciation of positivism comes from the philosophics. Not all of their criticisms refer to the research-relevant aspects of positivism. Often the label "positivist" serves as a catch-all category, as did empiricism, for their objections to mainstream social science and to capitalist society in general. Sometimes their critique relates to Comte's political philosophy rather than to the modern version of positivism outlined above. Thus, the philosophics argue that positivism has an inherent conservative political bias; it obstructs change, it protects elites who use social science to dominate and oppress (Antonio and Piran, 1978:2), it supports the status quo (Marcuse, 1956:349), and it advances the ends of imperialism in general. It is insensitive to the priority which the philosophics accord to humanism, the creative individual, self-realization (Agger, 1976:20), dialectics, egalitarianism, and transcendental truth (Van Den Berg, 1980:451).

The philosophics are equally unhappy with the research-relevant aspects of positivist epistemological tenets. They reject efforts to integrate natural and social science, arguing that human beings are set off from the rest of nature and must be studied with methods qualitatively different from those of the natural sciences. The philosophics contend that social science is superior to natural science, but they reject social inquiry in the form of contemporary social science derived from physical science. They are critical of natural science because it is based on direct impressions of reality (appearances that are distorted in capitalist society) and cannot see beneath the surface. It looks at events in a piecemeal, fragmented fashion, excludes history and process (Appelbaum, 1978:76), and rejects the idea of contradiction and antagonism (Lukacs, 1971:10). It is one-sidedly materialist and misses the totality (McLellan, 1975:58). Because positivism employs a natural science point of view to study people, it reduces all knowledge to biological responses (Kolakowski, 1972:18); it uses impersonal methods, "statistical summations, correlations, and other manipulations" (Lee, 1975:47), and machines to study humans (Agger, 1976:20). This does an "injustice to the role of consciousness and the capacity of men to radically transform their life-situation and actualize their aims or projects" (Bandyopadhyay, 1971:10).

Because positivism requires that research results be tested, the philosophics argue that it is too concerned with petty details and empirical verification (Antonio and Piran, 1978) and that it assumes the "facts speak for themselves" (Horton and Filsoufi, 1977:9). The positivist assumptions about value-neutral research and the distinction between facts and values are equally offensive to the philosophics.

The deductivists, especially Stalin, offer criticisms of positivism that parallel those of the philosophics. The deductivists identify positivism closely with Western social science and reject both as do the philosophics. In addition, they denounce positivism as incompatible with their understanding of the dialectic as quite abstract and even metaphysical in character. Today the critique of positivism by modern deductivists such as Igor Naletov (1984) in the USSR is as strong as ever and much more sophisticated than that traditionally offered by the Stalinists.

The deductivists disagree with most elements of positivism. They object to its emphasis on concrete reality and the importance of empirical data in testing theory. The deductivists see natural and social science as unified under dialectical materialism, but they maintain that the two are different. Social science can never be as rigorous as natural science because it is more complex. The deductivists also question the possibility of a value-free research and the positivist distinction between facts and values.

### The Structuralist Marxists: Partial Positivists

The structuralist Marxists are also hostile to positivism. But they object very little to the assimilation of natural science with social science (Althusser, 1965:177) because they believe the two are similar and have a "dialectical unity." Neither are they bothered very much by the positivist's emphasis on the distinction between facts and values. However, the assumption that rigorous research is based on direct observation of reality and requires testing against evidence poses real problems for the structuralists. They complain that positivism reduces theory construction "to a process of empirical generalization of law-like regularities" (Wright, 1978:10). It is based on existing categories of reality which, for the structuralists, implies support for the status quo. In short, the structuralists contend that Marxists cannot be positivists, but, unlike the philosophics, they do not disagree with all of the elements of positivism.

### Materialist Marxists: Qualified Positivists

Of all the Marxists the materialists come closest to accepting positivism. The precursors of today's materialists, such as the Austro-Marxists (except for Max Adler) and the Marxists of the Second

International, were almost uniformly sympathetic to it (Bottomore, 1968; Bottomore and Goode, 1978). In fact, a number of epistemological elements are common to both the materialists' views and to positivism. They agree on the empirical character of systematic rigorous research. Both accept the unity of natural and social science (Bottomore, 1975), the similarity of the methods employed by each, and the potentially objective character of research. This follows from their view that man is part of nature rather than different in character (Bukharin, 1925). They distinguish between the content of value statements and normative conclusions (Bottomore, 1975). The materialists do not assume that positivism inherently requires a neglect of theory. They do not deny that certain positivists take facts at face value, ignore the context in which data are gathered, or violate the scientific character of investigation. They argue that there is nothing intrinsic in a positivist perspective which necessarily leads to these poor research practices; the abuses of some positivists do not constitute grounds for a return to speculation or introspection as methods of inquiry. Although the materialists offer a scathing critique of Comte's positivism and its political assumptions, they do not reject it *in toto*. They sort out what they find useful in it and discard what is not valuable to them.

The main point on which the materialists take issue with positivist principles involves the claim that research must be value-neutral. As argued above, this criticism of one aspect of positivism does not necessarily constitute a point of disagreement with contemporary social science.

### Positivism: A Summary

In this section positivism was described and Marxist views of positivism were compared to see which were in agreement with those elements of positivism essential to the production of defensible research. As was the case with the other research-relevant epistemological assumptions examined in this chapter, the materialists come closest to the view widely accepted by the social science community. They are qualified positivists, sympathetic to the most important elements of positivism: the unity of social and natural science, the necessity to test research conclusions, and the distinction between the content of normative and empirical statements. The philosophics were shown to reject positivism in its entirety. The deductivists criticize almost every element of positivism. The structuralists are more critical of positivism than the materialists, but they still can be labelled partial positivists because they accept a certain number of elements central to it. All Marxists object to the positivist principles that research should be completely value-free and that the researcher should be absolutely "neutral." We now turn to a consideration of how the Marxists line up on the epistemological assumptions related to objectivity.

### OBJECTIVITY

Objectivity is another central epistemological assumption of the generally accepted view of research. To be objective is to consider reality without the distortions resulting from personal preferences or prejudices. Objectivity refers to being able to discover the qualities and relations of a subject matter as they exist independently of an inquirer's thoughts and desires about them. Objectivists contend that by "careful use of our perceptual organs and our reasoning ability we can arrive at beliefs about things as they actually are. This results from agreement between observers on the non-value characteristics of what is observed" (Cunningham, 1973a; 1975). Objectivity implies a distinction between the cognizing subject and the object of cognition, between the researcher and what is being studied.

Objectivity does not deny that observations can be deformed or inaccurate. From the point of view of contemporary social science research, this only means that objectivity is difficult, not that it is impossible.

Marxists are divided on the question of objectivity and the possibility of objective research. Some, like the materialists, are quite committed to it, whereas others, like the philosophics, see it as an illusion or as class-based. The deductivists and the structuralists adopt qualified, compromise positions on objectivity.

#### Objectivity Is an Illusion or a Matter of Class
#### Consciousness: The Philosophics

As far as the philosophic Marxists are concerned, the research enterprise of contemporary social sciences has no special claim to objectivity, no exceptional techniques of investigation, no monopoly on truth. There are two views on objectivity within philosophic Marxism. Some of the philosophics conclude that there are absolutely no privileged objective statements. Reality and one's knowledge of it are subjective. A second group links objectivity to a working-class perspective.

The largest group of philosophics claims that any so-called objective reality is merely a construction that functions in the interests of the bourgeoisie. They argue that this objective world must be overthrown. For the philosophics the object of knowledge is not material but ideal. They restore philosophical analysis and subjectivity to an equal footing with those forms of inquiry valued by contemporary social science. Speculation, intuition, personal feelings, emotions, and experiences are a means to truth. Relativism and subjectivism promise knowledge, based on personal consciousness, which is superior to rigorous sytematic research and its claims of objectivity.

These philosophics doubt the possibility of objectivity, grounded on empirical evidence as defined within contemporary social science. They have several reasons for their stance. They say that facts, which serve as the basis for objectivity, by their very existence imply an interpretation and are relative (Lukacs, 1971:5). Human experience is unique. Knowledge is created in the mind of the researcher and does not exist in an extra-mental state. The true nature of social relationships in a capitalist system is said to be camouflaged or distorted by misleading appearances. This is discussed further in the next chapter in connection with observation. The way those undertaking research see the world is not objective but instead is colored by the dominant historical patterns of our times (i.e., capitalism). Knowledge cannot be objective but is necessarily historically relative. These philosophics argue that Marxism requires that they reject neutrality, and this in turn implies a rejection of objectivity. Objectivity requires a consensus between researchers who agree as to what they see and feel. This is impossible as far as the philosophics are concerned.

Objectivity assumes a distinct subject, that is, person who stands apart from society and observes the object. For the philosophics this is also impossible. The subject and object of inquiry are fused, linked by their common humanity. Researchers are in and of society.

The mind of the researcher perceives itself in the subject studied. The researcher is both the person-subject and the human-object of investigation.

A second group within philosophic Marxism argues in favor of a form of "objectivity" based on consciousness and linked to social class. Only the working class, these philosophics tell us, has the ability and motivation to understand the totality objectively. As Lukacs puts it, "the proletariat *always aspires towards the truth* even in its 'false' consciousness and in its substantive errors" (1971:72). The perspective of the revolutionary class or the proletariat is said to be superior to that of any other class, more objective in each historical period because it is the only one capable of speaking for the process of change (Schaff, 1971:193–94; 326). First, the proletariat is said to be the class that is on the rise, approaching power. Its perspective is therefore superior to that of all other classes. Second, the proletariat is believed to be the "last class" to assume power. This is based on Marx's expectation that the proletarian victory will end class struggle. The proletarian is the standard of the future. Third, the objective self-interest of the proletariat is defined as being synonymous with that of the whole of society (Lukacs, 1971:42). Because it is the only class in this unique position, its perspective is assumed to be clearer and more objective than that of all other classes (Lowy, 1973:230–34).

## Objectivity Is a Possibility: The Materialists

Historically, the materialist Marxists, including the Austro-Marxists, many members of the Second International, Georgy Plekhanov, and Nikolai Bukharin, have been strict objectivists holding that knowledge is not entirely dependent on consciousness. Although they reject the neutrality implied by positivism, they do not consider commitment or value judgment to be incompatible with objectivity (Sztompka, 1979b:221). The successors of these early materialists argue that researchers can be partial to the interests of the proletariat and the popular classes and remain objective. Indeed, they say that because they are not neutral it is even more essential that they be as objective as possible. They argue, first, that they must be objective in order to advance the particular interest of the proletariat. Next, they contend it is a disservice to one's goals to deform reality or interpret it falsely with the intention of "aiding" the proletariat. This can only have negative consequences. Values should not lead one to deform what one observes in reality. The modern materialists acknowledge that many things limit the possibility of absolute objectivity. Efforts are sometimes made to conceal and mystify reality. Critical information may be systematically withheld. But the materialists remain committed, in principle, to objectivity.

For the materialists, accepting the goal of objectivity does not require that any special status be accorded to a particular class perspective. They criticize those who say that only the working class can be objective because this is a class-relativist position that assumes the existence of a "clear sightedly revolutionary proletariat" (Collier, 1973:14). They point out that this view cannot account for false consciousness or the mistakes made by the working class in the past. Knowledge cannot be considered "true" because it is associated with a specific class.

The materialists, unlike the philosophics, accept that the object and subject of inquiry can be distinct, at least for purposes of inquiry. This implies that the researcher can separate the self from the situation being studied, at least enough to achieve a certain measure of objectivity.

### Objectivity by Self-Attribution: The Deductivist and Structuralist Marxists

The deductivists and the structuralists consider objectivity to be important and argue for the objectivity of their respective points of view. The deductivists do not, however, associate objectivity with rigorous research (Kelle and Makeshin, 1977–79), nor do they require it to be based on observable experience. They maintain that dialectical materialism and "scientific socialism" provide an objective view of the world. In the most extreme form they contend that the laws governing society were discovered by Marx and Engels and need only be studied, understood, and applied to guarantee objectivity. They assume that their point of view represents that of the working class.

The structuralists are also self-declared objectivists in the same sense as the deductivists. They oppose subjectivism, arguing that their Marxist structuralist method is scientific and, therefore, that it assures objectivity. But care is warranted here for, although they are favorable to objectivity in principle, their definition of it, inspired by Althusser, is not the same as that in common use. As a result, many structuralists depart substantially from the view of objectivity implicit within contemporary social science.

Althusser argues that everyone "reads" objective material from a unique and particular perspective. This implies a certain relativism. The goal of objectivity itself is called into question by the assumption that knowledge is acquired subjectively, by one's personal logic or problematic, or from one's sociohistorical standpoint (Meszaros, 1972:65). For the Althusserians, a conceptual framework is not objective because it is a "more or less adequate reflection of reality," but rather because it is "determinant" of how reality is viewed (Cunningham, 1977:109). Althusser's conception of "scientific research" cannot be objective in the normal sense in which this word is used in terms of the generally accepted model because it rejects testing or reference to external evidence. The case for "structuralist objectivity" rests on internal intellectual consistency alone.

Althusser and the structuralists reject, as do the materialists, any suggestion that objectivity is associated with social class position, that is, the superiority of the working-class perspective.

The structuralists agree with the philosophics in that they also consider the subject and object of research not as "entities, but as relationships one to the other." That is, they consider the subject and object to be linked; they see the subject as both structuring and being structured by the object (Harvey, 1973:298). The structuralists argue that, if one distinguishes strictly between the subject and the object of research, one attributes too much importance to the particular roles of individuals, thus once again violating the structuralists' assumption that individuals are of no special significance (Althusser, 1965:25). The difference between the structuralists and the philosophics is that the philosophics ground their view of object-subject relations in humanism, whereas the structuralists regard humanist statements about a subject and an object as mere emotionalism and sentimentalism and therefore as of no value. In any case, both the subject and object disappear and have no importance when examined from a structuralist point of view.

### Objectivity and Research

Contemporary social science research requires that the researcher at least make an effort to be objective. Such attempts, of course, are no guarantee of objectivity. But to cease even to strive to be objective leaves one in a position of absolute subjectivity, unacceptable in terms of the norms of modern social science. The philosophics reject efforts at being objective, contending that objectivity itself is merely an illusion. One group of philosophics is not in the least uncomfortable with the subjective character of their own research and thus they set themselves and their research apart from the norms of the generally accepted research model. A second group of philosophics attributes objectivity to a class position. Their perspective assumes *a priori* that the proletariat is objective and that other classes are subjective. Few who do not share their assumptions would agree with this view. Research on the superiority of working-class objectivity might in fact show that the proletariat is indeed enlightened in a special way. But it might also demonstrate that workers are subject to "false consciousness"or that they have made serious mistakes in assessing reality in the past. The objectivity of the proletariat in the future, therefore, remains problematic and cannot be accepted with certainty.

The structuralist and deductivist Marxists call for objectivity. But they are objective in terms of self-definition rather than in the sense assumed by contemporary social science. This has the effect of limiting the acceptability of their research to a relatively narrow audience.

The materialists' view of objectivity closely parallels that of the generally accepted understanding of research. They maintain that objectivity is a goal for research. As far as they are concerned, there is no inconsistency in their simultaneous rejection of neutrality and their commitment to objectivity. They deny that objectivity is inherently linked to a special class perspective. They are not troubled by the fact that accepting objectivity implies recognition that the object and subject of inquiry can be distinct from each other.

## RESEARCH IMPLICATIONS OF MARXIST
## EPISTEMOLOGICAL ASSUMPTIONS: SUMMARY

Logic and consistency suggest that Marxists are oriented toward certain kinds of research by their epistemological views. Specific epistemological assumptions facilitate carrying out research in terms of contemporary social science norms while others make it almost impossible. In this chapter it has been argued that among the Marxists the materialists are those whose views are closest to this generally accepted model. This means that their research results and the knowledge they produce can be defended within these terms of reference and can serve as a basis for intervention with respect to the policymaking model. The philosophic Marxists consistently make epistemological assumptions that are idealist, subjectivist, and radically incompatible with those of the generally accepted model of research outlined in Chapter 1. The deductivists defend epistemological positions in some of the same ways and also diverge from the norms of contemporary social science research. The structuralists reject many of the epistemological norms of this generally accepted model, but certain of their views are not incompatible with it.

To review the details of this chapter, it has been suggested that the materialists are in general agreement with philosophical materialism rather than idealism, which influences their other research-relevant epistemological assumptions such as their theory of knowledge. They are determinists; they reject both fatalism and voluntarism. They emphasize the importance of analysis, that is, the study of the parts in order to learn about the whole. They tend to advocate what has been described here as general empiricism rather than classical empiricism, though some of these tend toward crude empiricism. They accept those aspects of positivism essential to contemporary social science research (the unity of natural and social science, the testability of theory with data, the substantive difference between empirical and normative statements). The elements of positivism which they reject are not essential to contemporary research (the value neutrality of research and the nonpartisanship of the person undertaking inquiry). The materialists recognize the importance of objectivity while agreeing that it cannot be perfectly achieved.

Although the congruence of the materialists' epistemological positions with those of the general model does not guarantee that they will produce research acceptable in terms of contemporary social science, it does increase the probability that this will be the case. Their epistemological views facilitate their undertaking studies that produce results of use in defending their knowledge claims, which can be used as a basis for action, and that will be of interest to a broader audience including many non-Marxists. The same cannot be said for the other kinds of Marxists.

The philosophics' research-related epistemological assumptions are influenced by their idealism. Many of them accept that knowledge is a construct of the mind. They are voluntarists; almost all of them are anti-determinist. They emphasize the idea that free will, rather than social factors, influences human action and consciousness. In their view, the totality is overwhelmingly significant and so different in kind from the sum of the parts that the study of the parts can tell us little about the whole. They are hostile to both crude empiricism and to general empiricism. Some of them are favorable to an idealist form of empiricism called classical empiricism. But in its classical form, empiricism is incompatible with the requirements of contemporary social science, and, therefore, subscribing to it does not encourage the philosophics to produce research acceptable in terms of the generally accepted model. The philosophics are hostile to all aspects of positivism, including those elements of it essential to the production of testable research findings. They either embrace subjectivism, rejecting all possibility of objectivity, or they see objectivity as linked to a special class perspective. In the latter case the working-class point of view is assumed to be more objective than that of any other social class. The epistemological commitments of these Marxists, as with the others, affect their choice of methods, how they understand science, and how they carry out research. Non-Marxists who agree with the generally accepted model are unlikely to find research undertaken by the philosophics and based on these generally idealist assumptions of much interest.

The deductivists are in much the same situation as the philosophics in terms of their research-relevant epistemological assumptions. In short, they reject many of the views central to contemporary social science research. They have a mixed theory of knowledge, and they advocate a contradictory combination of fatalism and voluntarism rather than determinism. They attribute great importance to the totality, and at the same time, they oppose empiricism and positivism in all forms. While arguing in favor of objectivity, they define it in a way that is not generally accepted, that is, as mere consistency with the writings of the founders of Marxism.

Many of the structuralists' epistemological assumptions appear to be close to those of the generally accepted model while others are inconsistent with it. Guided by Althusser, their views are a combination of elements drawn from idealism and materialism. Their theory of knowledge is mixed. They are philosophical materialists in the sense that they advocate structural determinism and reject voluntarism. They are favorable to objectivity, at least in the abstract. They propose that the study of the parts is neither absolutely essential to understanding the totality nor completely irrelevant. They are not hostile to all the elements of positivism accepting its assimilation of natural and social science and the substantive difference between empirical and normative statements. But they also hold certain epistemological views that are philosophically idealist and that contradict the assumptions of the generally accepted model. They reject empiricism in all forms and those elements of positivism that require research results be tested, directly or indirectly, against observable evidence. Although they insist that inquiry be objective, as required by contemporary social science, they define objectivity in a special manner, not as reflecting a state that exists in the real world but rather as "determining" a point of view about reality. The research-relevant epistemological assumptions of the structuralists constitute a creative, though contradictory, attempt to synthesize epistemological idealism and materialism.

Among the Marxists, the structuralists occupy an intermediate position between the materialists on one side and the deductivists and philosophics on the other. This element of variety within the structuralists' epistemological views provides the basis, as will be seen in Chapter 5, for enabling some of them to undertake research in line with the norms of contemporary social science and, therefore, of interest to a broader audience.

Although epistemological assumptions exert an important influence on the quality of research for all the Marxists, they do not determine its defensibility alone. It would be premature to conclude that certain Marxist groups do not undertake research of interest in terms of the generally accepted model solely because of the incompatibility of their epistemological orientations with those of the generally accepted model. An examination of the methodological assumptions of the various types of Marxists will provide additional evidence as to which share views in common with contemporary social science on these questions that underlie research and provide a basis for the production of knowledge useful for policymaking.

# 3.

## THE METHODOLOGICAL ASSUMPTIONS OF RESEARCH: MARXIST VIEWS

This chapter (1) compares and evaluates the views of the various Marxist groups concerning the methodological assumptions needed to undertake research that is valuable according to the criteria of contemporary social science and to produce knowledge useful as a basis for action; and (2) illustrates the links between Marxists' epistemological choices, outlined in Chapter 2, and their methodological options.

Methodology tells us how to go about acquiring knowledge, but not specifically what to expect to find in the real world. It concerns the instruments and procedures needed for research. The Marxists' assumptions about methodology influence their research and strengthen or weaken their knowledge claims. Methodology provides the link between the epistemological positions described in the previous chapter and the actual research practice described in Chapter 5.

The norms of contemporary social inquiry are relatively precise about methodology. Within the research process observation precedes the formulation of new theory; therefore, induction has priority over deduction. Theory must conform to data rather than the reverse. It is in this sense that research has a concrete rather than an abstract beginning. Concepts must be clear and defined in real terms, linked to adequate indicators, measured accurately and reliably. Observation and interpretation should be carried out so that the resulting data provide the evidence needed for theory construction and testing. If theory is to be relevant for policymaking, it must be formulated in terms of causal explanatory forms, constructed on the basis of real concepts, grounded in reality, and tested by application.

Overall, the methodological assumptions of the materialist Marxists conform more closely to the requirements of contemporary social science than do those of the other Marxists, chiefly because they are empirically constrained. The methodological assumptions of the philosophic, structuralist, and deductivist Marxists are less likely to require reference to observable experience. *The philosophics' general method is best described as interpretive and dialectical, that of the structuralists as "scientific" abstraction* (Althusser, 1971:75), *and that of the deductivists as a priori (deductive) analysis.* (See Table 2.)

Although the research process may be regarded as inductive or deductive (or both), or as initially focusing on concrete data or abstract theory, it is the materialist Marxists who emphasize induction and argue that data be given priority in the preliminary stages of the research process.

To be defensible in terms of contemporary social science norms, research must be based on direct or indirect observation, and only the materialists are optimistic about the utility of such observation. They agree that interpretation is part of the research process and that different interpretations may exist as long as they are not contradictory. But unlike other Marxists, the materialists insist that such inconsistencies need to be resolved by reference to directly or indirectly observable experience. The other Marxists see interpretation as a subjective, almost arbitrary process without reference to observation of the real world.

Modern social science assumes that both data and concepts are used to produce theory. Concepts must be defined in real terms, and indicators must be available to set out the limits and use of concepts. In contrast, most of the structuralist, deductivist, and philosophic Marxists contend that data are either irrelevant or invented in the sense of being arbitrary. Their concepts tend to be defined nominally rather than in real terms. Only the materialist Marxists argue for the use of concepts defined in real terms and linked by observation to concrete indicators.

Marxists use causal, dialectical, or teleological explanatory forms for the rules that constitute their theories. The causal explanatory

**Table 2**
**Marxist Methodological Assumptions: Summary Statement for Chapter 3**

| Method | Materialists | Structuralists | Philosophics | Deductivists |
|---|---|---|---|---|
| Research Method | Largely the same as contemporary social science | "Scientific" abstraction | Interpretative and dialectical | Deduction |
| Research Process | Priority to data and induction | Anti-induction Priority to theory | Anti-induction Priority to theory | Deductive Priority to theory |
| Observation | Useful | Not useful | Not useful Limited to appearance | Not useful |
| Interpretation | Constrained by real world | Unconstrained by reality Inconsistent interpretations possible | Unconstrained Inconsistent interpretations possible | All interpretation follows from dialectical and historical materialism This theory has special status |
| Data | Reflect reality | Of no use in social analysis Theory reflects reality but data do not | Arbitrary creation of human mind | Data are of secondary import Dialectical and historical materialism is most important for understanding the world |

**Table 2**
*(Continued)*

| Method | Materialists | Structuralists | Philosophics | Deductivists |
|---|---|---|---|---|
| Concepts | Defined in real terms<br>Seek indicators for concepts | All nominal<br>No indicators | Nominal<br>No indicators | Real and nominal<br>Indicators unnecessary |
| **Explanatory Forms** | | | | |
| Causality | Direct causality ok | Structuralist causality<br>Oppose direct causality | Hegelian causality<br>Direct causality opposed | *A priori* causality |
| Dialectic and teleology | Reject the dialectic or define it concretely as research aid which does not exclude causality | Some effort to reconcile dialectic and structuralist causality<br>Reject direct causality | Abstract dialectic and teleology presented as replacing direct causality | Dialectical materialism<br>Reject direct causality<br>Reject formal logic |
| **Theory** | | | | |
| Construction | On basis of data and observation | Form of intellectual work<br>No role for data and observation | Personal, subjective experience<br>No role for data or observation<br>On basis of working-class experience | *A priori*<br>Reason from historical materialism to new topic |

56

| | | | | |
|---|---|---|---|---|
| Testing | Test theory against evidence based on data and observation in concrete reality | Evaluation of theory on basis of internal characteristics, of consistency and logic but not on basis of data or observation | Intuition and introspection serve as substitutes for testing<br><br>Political criteria, i.e., serves the working class | Test them against pregiven tenets and against historical events (USSR 1917)<br><br>Data and observation unimportant |
| Application | Practice is theory application for correction, a form of testing theory | No application necessary<br><br>Practice is intervention in the theoretical realm | Praxis is human development, not application of theory or testing it | Practice is application of historical-materialism, not testing or applying theory |

form is central to the generally accepted model of research, and essential in the policymaking perspective. But only the materialists either accept the notion of direct causality and/or define the dialectic so that it does not exclude causal explanatory forms. None of the Marxists, except the materialists, understands theory in the sense required by contemporary social science. Only the materialists conceive of practice as the application of theory, grounded in research, to real world situations, as a means of correcting and refining it.

## THE RESEARCH PROCESS: DEDUCTION VERSUS INDUCTION

Contemporary social science research, as outlined in Chapter 1, emphasizes the inductive aspect of inquiry. Induction involves generalizing from particular observations and testing results. Deduction amounts to accepting a generalized statement, examining its implications, and then applying the principle. Deduction is an important part of the process of inquiry but only for exploring conclusions, not for generating them. Research cannot be said to "begin" with data or theory in an absolute sense because it is almost always initiated in an ongoing system, that is, data are collected in the context of some preexisting theoretical framework. Theory in turn is contingent on previous observations and theories. But the general practice of contemporary social science emphasizes "beginning" research with data in the sense that observation precedes formulation (which usually means reformulation) of theory. All these aspects of the research process are interrelated and will be treated together here.

Most Marxists discuss these questions only indirectly, by reference to their respective interpretations of Marx's method. Because most maintain that only their own methodological options are inspired by Marx's example, this discussion of the research process will necessarily focus on how contemporary Marxist groups interpret Marx's methodology. As it turns out, the deductivists, philosophics, and structuralists generally view the research process as beginning at the theoretical level and proceeding deductively. More in line with contemporary social science, the materialists emphasize induction and a concrete beginning for research.

Althusser and the other structuralist Marxists regard Marx's method as theoretical abstraction. They therefore reject induction as a methodological procedure, arguing that research begins with the general, the abstract-in-thought, and then proceeds to scientific knowledge which is concrete-in-thought (Althusser, 1976b:153–54; 1965:182–92; Althusser and Balibar, 1968:309). For the structuralists the concrete-in-thought does not refer to empirical reality. On the contrary, it is located within what they call the "general," at a still higher level of abstraction.

Most of the philosophic Marxists agree with the structuralists that Marx's method begins at the level of theory and involves deducing implications from some more general theoretical propositions. The starting point of inquiry for these Marxists cannot be a concrete reality that refers only to scattered, isolated data that are inherently suspect, imperfect forms of information. As was shown in Chapter 2, these Marxists are concerned with the totality, and in their view it must be grasped at the theoretical level or not at all.

A few of the philosophics say that Marx's method was to start with "the concrete" (Lefebvre, 1969b; Horton, 1972:28; Sartre, 1963; Markovic, 1974). But they criticize Marx for doing so, charging that it is an imperfect, incomplete beginning because it deals only with the apparent, everyday experience, the obvious. Only in the later stages of research, they tell us, did Marx go on to discover the real, complex concrete. But as with the structuralists, this final, authentic "concrete," which some philosophics take for their goal exists only at the abstract level.

The deductivists understand Marx's method to be expressed in historical materialism and dialectical materialism. The propositions of both are assumed to be self-evident. Through reason and logic, the deductivists extract from historical materialism a general explanation of the world around them which they then apply to specific cases. They see no need to compare the theory's expectations with reality (Fischer, 1966:127; Ukraintsev, 1978:97–98). This becomes a purely deductive, *a priori* approach to inquiry. It is the central defining characteristic of their method. Many of them reject induction as a methodological procedure, claiming it is "overused" in research today (Medvedev, 1969:22, 58).

The materialists hold that Marx's method requires a moving back and forth from the concrete to the theoretical, but it begins with the concrete. They describe Marx's method of alternating between induction and deduction as "successive approximations" beginning with "the movement from the empirical to the abstract, consisting of a period of preliminary observation, empirical study and tentative interpretation leading to ... abstraction." The "second procedure of the method then takes place in the step-by-step transition from the abstract theory ... to the concrete by successive approximations in which one ... reconstructs the theory to make it more conditional and complex" (McQuarie, 1978:222–23). By successively refining and adding more variables, a closer approximation to reality is achieved. A number of materialists emphasize that Marx's method implies a continuing, never complete, dynamic, overall method of this character (McQuarie, 1978:228–31; Howard and King, 1975; Larionov, 1970). This is consistent with their epistemological assumptions that the study of the parts contributes to knowledge of the whole.

In general, then, the structuralists and philosophics view Marx's method as consistent with their epistemological idealism and anti-empiricism. In the best of circumstances they begin with the theoretical, the abstract, with ideas, and later proceed to the "concrete." Often what they refer to as concrete simply represents well-honed abstract theoretical presentations. At its worst the idea or abstraction generates its own concrete manifestations that are assumed to be valid, independent of testing. This form of *a priori* deduction is incompatible with the canons of contemporary inquiry. The deductivists' approach to deduction and induction in the research process suffers from the same fatal weakness.

On the other hand, the materialists have epistemological views, empiricist and positivist, which are compatible with a concrete beginning for research and with induction rather than deduction (Larionov, 1970:82). Theory guides data collection, but theory is in turn subject to testing against data. This is consistent with the generally accepted approach to inquiry.

## OBSERVATION: GOING BEYOND APPEARANCES

Methodological assumptions about observation are directly related to the selection of research techniques and, ultimately, the quality of the results produced. It is through observation that we learn, indirectly, about external reality. Observation does not duplicate the external or real world. On the contrary, observation requires selection and an effort to aggregate and integrate what is pertinent for the question under study. Observation produces data that serve as storehouses of information. It is through observation that concepts are formulated. Observation is meaningless without a commitment to objectivity and the procedures that encourage it. The problem in the social sciences is that appearances can be deceptive, and one must often look below the surface to discover what is really happening. If observation is superficial or distorted, it cannot contribute to the production of knowledge.

Marx was particularly sensitive to the danger of not going beyond appearances. He saw reality as inevitably hidden and disguised from everyday view in the capitalist system. He insisted that research methods go beyond superficial forms to study the actual content of phenomena. His comments on these matters have influenced Marxists' views of observation right down to the present. Marxists use a number of different terms to express this dichotomy between what can be observed directly and what can be understood by looking below the surface.

| First View | What Is Really Out There |
| --- | --- |
| Observed forms | Disguised relationships |
| Illusion | Reality |
| Form | Content |
| Simple form of manifestation | Inner connections |
| Phenomenal forms | Actual forms—real relations |
| Nonessential relations | Essential relations |
| Phenomena (visible) | Hidden substratum |
| Appearances | Essence |

No matter what terms are used, all Marxists take Marx's warning seriously. They agree on the necessity to go beyond appearances, but they disagree on how easily this can be done and how to do it. We will see that most of the Marxists are excessively pessimistic about the value of observation in the context of research. *The*

*materialists, however, do consider that observable experience can*
*contribute to the production of knowledge.*

### Observation Rejected

The philosophics are dubious about the possibility that rigorous observation can move inquiry beyond the realm of appearances. As they see it, "that which is, cannot be true" (Bloch, 1961:65). This is in part the result of their epistemological views which are sympathetic to idealism. But it also results from their understanding of reality as a construction dependent on mental processes. Reality is only an appearance; the essence rests within the mind, and it cannot be revealed by observation. Their opposition to positivism and general empiricism, combined with their enthusiasm for classical idealist empiricism, reinforces their skepticism about the value of observation as does their view that objectivity is either impossible or class-related.

In addition, the philosophics maintain that observation is distorted by the processes of reification and fetishism. Marxists use these terms to refer to mechanisms that exist under capitalism to conceal what is really going on in the world. For example, social relationships come to look as if they are impersonal, objective relations, governed by natural laws rather than artificially imposed by capitalism. What seems to be happening in bourgeois society, surface appearances, is not indicative of what is actually going on (Marx, 1973:247). There is a gap between underlying reality and what is directly observed. The philosophics contend that observation is limited to the visible, empirical level and is, therefore, by definition, superficial and systematically misleading because the world is characterized by mystification, domination, and false consciousness. According to these Marxists, observation cannot uncover reality, the essence, the hidden substratum (Lukacs, 1971).

For the deductivists, too, immediate observation has only limited value, at least under capitalism when it offers an imperfect form of knowledge, especially for the social sciences. They emphasize the necessity of going beyond initial observations to detect inner relations and connections (Cornforth, 1963:32–34). This can be accomplished, they tell us, only with the guidance of Marx's theory, that is, historical materialism and dialectical materialism.

The structuralists take even more seriously the need to go beyond appearances to underlying realities. Like the philosophics and deductivists, they feel that reality is hidden and distorted as a result of the process of reification (Althusser and Balibar, 1968:313). They argue that the underlying structural configurations that interest them and constitute the building blocks of the real world can be studied only indirectly through their effects. Abstraction or systematic "theoretical labor," not observation, is required to uncover their dynamic.

Among the structuralists, Althusser is notable for even further complicating the problem of discovering hidden reality. First, he claims that observation is useless since knowledge is theoretical, involving the "reproduction of the concrete by way of thought." Then he asserts that even those who abandon observation and employ theoretical analysis in order to go beyond surface appearances will inevitably fail. It is not the "interior" that is important but the "concept-of-the-interior," for knowledge of the "inner aspect" always remains hidden, "enclosed in an empiricism and an empirical state of mind" (Althusser and Balibar, 1968:190–91). Later, he abandoned this absolutist position (in a self-criticism published in English in 1976) while still maintaining that observation is useless for producing knowledge. For Althusser there is a "paradoxical identity of non-vision and vision within vision itself" (Althusser and Balibar, 1968:21).

### Observation Accepted

The materialist Marxists do not consider the problem of going beyond appearances to be insurmountable as do the other Marxists. They argue that direct or indirect observation may yield valuable information about the external world. They suggest that an astute observer can distinguish between illusion and reality, between form and content, between the nonessential and the essential. Social reality certainly may be hidden, and one may have to look at what lies beneath the everyday, the commonplace, but for the materialists the approach taken by contemporary social science does permit one to go beyond the superficial. The materialists are optimistic about the possibility of overcoming the analytical problems posed by fetishism and reification without denying that certain individuals, even those formally committed to systematic inquiry, may deform or distort what they observe. Self-interest may cause one to view things in terms that flatter one's own role and perpetuate one's advantage. For the materialists, this does not mean that observation as such is useless, but rather that its quality can vary and therefore must be examined.

### Implications for Research: Conclusion

The philosophic Marxists exaggerate the gap between appearances and essence. They argue that empirical, quantitative research is impossible because neither direct nor indirect observation can go beyond phenomenal forms. Both the deductivists and structuralists maintain the same position, although the epistemological basis for their rejection of observation in research is more complicated. They all conclude that reality cannot be known through systematic social science research. The implications of this position are dramatic and far reaching. Observation is essential to contemporary social science, serving as the means for separating what is acceptable from what is not. To the extent that results of research are untested against observable experience, they are likely to be of interest to few non-Marxists. *Only the materialists argue that careful direct or indirect observation can enable us to go beyond appearances in a defensible way.*

### INTERPRETATION

Interpretation is part of the process of research whereby meaning is attributed to data. All Marxists agree on the necessity to interpret data, but they do not agree on how the process of interpretation should be understood. *Many Marxists suggest that interpretation is a subjective, almost arbitrary process without an empirical referent in reality, such that the possibility of theory construction itself is called into question. The materialists, on the other hand, see interpretation as subject to constraint by comparison with the real world.*

Interpretation is central to the philosophics' method of inquiry. They say that each researcher creates his or her world through interpretation, attributing meaning to a reality that has no independent existence. For the philosophics, interpretation is not based on outside evidence in the form of data, nor is it concerned with discovering what is going on in an independent exterior reality. Rather, it results from sympathetic identification and empathy. According to the philosophics, this accounts for the differences among observers studying the same phenomenon. Many different pictures of the same collection of facts coexist. Even if two interpretations are inconsistent, it is not necessarily a question of one being right and the other wrong, or of one distorting the evidence and the other offering a true version. For the philosophics, such differences merely signal that the researchers in question have created their respective worlds differently. The choice among alternative views "is defined by a more general choice, one of a certain view of the world, which constitutes an integral part of historical interpretation" (Kolakowski, 1968:62). The philosophics' view of interpretation is consistent with their voluntarism and their rejection of any possibility of objectivity. Some of the philosophics do, however, argue for the superiority of what they call the "working-class" interpretation of events.

The structuralists agree with the philosophics, arguing that exterior data are subject to interpretation, in the sense that a number of different, even contradictory, "interpretations" of reality are defensible. But they maintain that their own interpretation, in terms of structures, is the only one that is objective and valid. Interpretation, as they view it, has no link to observable experience and is not constrained by reality.

The materialists regard interpretation as an effort to explain what data signify, to discover the meaning of relations that actually exist in the real world. It is a process that involves classification and leads to generalization and explanation (Kedrov and Spirkin, 1975:130). Certainly, interpretation in any instance is not self-evident, and there may be different interpretations of the same set of data, but the various interpretations should not conflict. Data can be manipulated or falsified, leading to an erroneous interpretation. But ultimately, if two different, inconsistent interpretations are presented, at least one must be wrong. Both cannot stand in the long term, if for no other reason than because in the presence of contradictory interpretations it would be impossible to produce data that could serve as a basis of knowledge. This view coincides with the materialists' determinism and their insistence that objectivity is a valid goal. The materialists' understanding of the process of interpretation parallels that of contemporary social science.

The deductivists argue that there can be only one interpretation of any set of data. But, for them, interpretation is automatic and follows directly from historical materialism's premises as a passive process of formal reasoning. This is consistent with their epistemological views, especially their argument that objectivity is possible only with a Marxist-Leninist framework. As with the philosophics and the structuralists, interpretations are not subject to testing in terms of being required to conform with concrete reality.

## DATA

Data, the most elementary form of information in research, result from observation and are the central building blocks of theory. Therefore, data are essential to contemporary social science research. *There are two views of data within Marxism. One sees data as simple creations of the human mind, constituted or invented in the sense of being arbitrary. The other understands data to reflect reality and to be of use in understanding what is going on in the real world.*

The philosophic Marxists' view of data is influenced by their anti-empiricism, their rejection of objectivity and of positivism, as well as their contention that observation is deformed under capitalism and can tell us nothing about the totality. Data, they say, are socially established, not collected but rather "produced" (Irvine, Miles, and Evans, 1979:3). Data are not just ascertained and studied in a scholarly fashion, rather, they are considered to be subjective raw materials waiting to be chiseled into shape. Under capitalism data are absolutely contaminated, mere expressions of exploitation and historical alienation. They are inhuman, impersonal, false, class biased, and determined by the social context within which they are collected. For the philosophics, knowledge must focus on the whole and the whole is distinct from data.

The structuralists also attribute little value to data. Because of their anti-empiricism, they concur with the philosophics that facts are conquered, constructed, and produced, unlikely to yield objective knowledge because they reflect only superficial appearances and because they are a function of the scientific practice employed to uncover them (Hindess and Hirst, 1975:3). Althusser relegates facts to his realm of "Generalities I," a form of imperfect knowledge, partly ideological and partly scientific, with no meaning outside of the problematic of past experience or past information which cannot help us understand what is happening at the moment (1965:182–95).

The deductivists' anti-empiricism and anti-positivism make them skeptical about the use of data in research. In addition, attention paid to data constitutes a risk that may bring them into conflict with the theoretical priority they accord to doctrine.

The materialist Marxists' view of data differs substantially from that of the other Marxists. They maintain that data are discovered through observation and that they are a potentially objective source of information about concrete reality. The materialists assert that data are to be studied, interpreted, and located in their sociohistorical context. Data in this context refer to the parts that constitute the whole or the totality. They are important in the description of reality and the construction and testing of theory. Mistakes may occur in collecting data and in its categorization; the recording of data may be biased. But despite these problems, and the necessity of critically assessing data, the potential objectivity and the usefulness of data in research are not called into question.

In sum, because of their understanding of data the philosophic Marxists are unlikely to produce research of interest to non-Marxists. If data are mere subjective creations of the human mind, any number of completely contradictory answers are appropriate for any given question, and systematic, generalizable research is not feasible. Few Marxists would disagree with the philosophics that all data collection (by means of observation) occurs in a social context and may be biased. But whereas the materialist Marxists feel that this raises problems for research, the others suggest that it eliminates any possibility of acquiring objective data.

## CONCEPTS AND INDICATORS

Concepts are the organizing instruments of empirical inquiry. They identify a class of things in the observed world that can be separated from the rest of the environment, defined, and treated as entities. Although the boundaries of a concept are imposed by the observer, they are not arbitrary because they are constrained by reality itself (Meehan, 1982:86). Two aspects of concepts are critical for the way Marxists view them: their definition in real or nominal terms and their measurement with indicators that establish value and tell us when they may be applied (Meehan, 1981:13, 48). Indicators are measured, and the measurement attributes the value taken by the variable which stands for the concept. At minimum, concepts should be closely related to indicators rather than remote from them and should be defined clearly rather than ambiguously.

Real definitions of concepts make reference to concrete experience. They are linked by observation to indicators, constrained by what goes on in the real world. Nominal definitions do not make reference to empirical observation, are not linked to indicators, and have no basis in observable reality. A concept defined nominally is merely a linguistic convention, an agreement to use a concept to stand for something else (Bierstedt, 1959). The meaning of such concepts can be assigned arbitrarily by the person using them because they serve only as symbols.

Nominally defined concepts are useful for some purposes, but they do not relate to the real world and cannot serve in statements that make assertions about empirical reality. If one wants to construct theories of use in policymaking, at least some concepts must be defined in real terms.

As we examine Marxist views of concepts, we will see that *the materialists emphasize real definitions of concepts and at the same time insist on indicators for the variables that stand for concepts as required by contemporary social science.* The philosophics and the structuralists prefer nominally defined concepts and reject any effort to link indicators to their concepts. The deductivists use a mix of concepts defined in real and nominal terms, but they show little interest in searching for indicators beyond those used by Marx himself in his initial formulation of his concepts.

Concepts, defined nominally, are central to the writings of the philosophic Marxists. They are uncomfortable with real concepts and suspicious of any claim, common in non-Marxist empirical social science research, that these concepts can be linked to indicators. The philosophics view real concepts as "partial," defending the values and interests of the researcher, reflecting the social situation within which they are constructed (Piccone, 1971:17–21). The philosophics prefer concepts defined nominally such as totalization, praxis, intention, and consciousness, which are remote from concrete empirical investigation. They do not require that their own concepts be related in any way to real conditions in the world around us (Hindess and Hirst, 1975:12). Philosophics seldom bother to link concepts to indicators. They do stress the importance of searching for the authentic, essential "meaning" of concepts, a task they see as wholly theoretical. In classic idealist fashion, the philosophics suggest that the meaning of a concept comes not from its use or by means of indicators, but rather through intellectual reflection.

The structuralists' concepts are exclusively nominal in character, intended, they say, to be "both universal and ahistorical" (Appelbaum, 1979). The concepts of overdetermination, displacement, condensation, contradiction, and structure-in-dominance are central to Althusser's theories. He says that such concepts cannot be "categories of the social world" because knowledge of a real object is not reached by immediate contact with the concrete but by the "production of the *concept* of that object (in the sense of object of knowledge) as the absolute condition of its *theoretical* possibility" (Althusser and Balibar, 1968:184). As a result, the meaning of his concepts is contained completely in their formal definitions. They are separate from the real world, without links to indicators (Castells and de Ipola, 1976).

The deductivists limit their analysis to concepts inherited from Marx or his successors such as Lenin. Some of their concepts are defined in real terms, and others in nominal terms, depending on the form in which they are "inherited." But like the structuralists and the philosophics, these Marxists show little interest in the possibility of employing indicators to link their concepts to measurement in today's world. They are satisfied that Marx assured the link to reality when he first formulated his own concepts.

The materialists attempt to give real definitions to at least some of their concepts such as forces-of-production, relations-of-production, and surplus value. They are preoccupied with linking them to the concrete with indicators, in measurable terms. They do not worry about a concept's intrinsic, "authentic" meaning in the existential sense as long as concepts make direct reference to reality; this facilitates the use of quantitative indicators.

In sum, only the materialist Marxists attempt to define at least some of their concepts in real terms and employ indicators for the variables that stand for them as required by contemporary social science. For the majority of the other Marxists, concepts are almost exclusively nominal and are used without reference to indicators, making it unlikely that research based on them would be acceptable from the point of view of the generally accepted model or useful in theories designed for policymaking purposes.

## EXPLANATORY FORMS: CAUSALITY, DIALECTICS, AND TELEOLOGY

The term "explanatory form" refers to the pattern of relationships among data observed in the world around us. Of the many possible explanatory forms available, only three will be discussed here because these are pertinent for the methodologies employed by Marxists and are consistently present in their theories: causality, dialectics, and teleology. Theories are composed of rules stated in terms of these explanatory forms. In this section we consider the character of explanatory forms. The methodological requirements of theories (construction, testing, and application) are discussed in the next section.

The rules or statements that make up theories could legitimately be expressed in terms of any number of explanatory forms. If, however, theory is to provide a basis for action and policymaking, rules with causal explanatory forms are required. If the rules or statements which make up a theory are not causal in form, intervention with predictable results is impossible (Meehan, 1981:86–87).

### Causality

Causal explanation implies that deliberately changing the value of one concept or variable in a theory will produce changes in the others according to known rules given specified limiting conditions (Meehan, 1982:105). A causal explanation, at its strongest, permits the researcher to say that a specific antecedent event (A) always produces, or determines, another equally specific event (B) given precisely defined conditions. Here (A) causes (B); (A) is a sufficient condition for (B). This is direct causality. In a weaker, yet still causal, form, (A) is a necessary condition for (B) to happen. By way of contrast, an association or correlation between two variables suggests that a link exists between them but that the character of the link remains unspecified. All that is known is that a certain percentage of the time an observed phenomenon will behave in a specific manner within known limits of error. The usefulness of this type of knowledge depends on the strength of the relationship between the two. If it is sufficiently high, it may provide a basis for prediction and even action. But because the mechanisms governing the relationship of the variables remain imprecise, it is impossible to systematically intervene to determine a given result all the time.

*Only the materialist Marxists accept causal explanation in terms recognized by contemporary social science, what is referred to here as direct causality.* Certain of the structuralists, philosophics, and deductivists reject causality altogether, while others seek to redefine it, sometimes in rather original ways. Thus, the philosophics speak of "Hegelian causality," the deductivists of "*a priori* causality," and the structuralists of "structural causality," but in each case what they offer as an alternative to direct causality is neither acceptable nor useful in the sense of contributing to isolating predictive relationships, nor is it convincing to non-Marxists whose methodology is grounded in the generally accepted model.

### Causality Adopted

The materialist Marxists define causality in the sense sketched out above and assumed by the generally accepted model of research. For them, society and nature are governed by laws that are causal in character (Bukharin, 1925:30). They argue that scientific prediction is of the following form: "under conditions X, Y, and Z, an entity A must behave in a manner M, unless the factors D, E, or F intervene, and then it must behave in a manner C" (Parekh, 1982:203–4). This view of causality is consistent with the materialists' view of determinism. It requires concrete investigation of reality compatible with their empiricism. It focuses on the parts rather than the abstract totality and uses information learned about the parts to understand the whole.

The materialists defend their understanding of direct causality against criticism from other Marxists who say it cannot be of use in studying change. Change, the materialists point out, is implicit within cause-effect relationships, though because of the way causal relations are represented—extracted momentarily from the larger complex of interconnections that constitute society—they may appear static (Oizerman, 1975:56–57).

The materialists have historically attributed priority to the economic (material conditions) as causative agents influencing the superstructure (social institutions in society). This is consistent with their view explained in Chapter 2 that the economic is the most important element of the whole. A problem results in both instances. If preference is attributed to the economic as a causal variable, without regard to what is going on in reality, the materialists risk falling into the error that is called economism, that is, the exaggeration of the importance of economic factors relative to other factors. But at least for those materialists whose research is of interest to non-Marxists, the commitment to the generally accepted view of causality takes precedence over any theoretical predisposition toward economic variables in instances where research shows they are of little importance. Priority to economic variables must be a matter of hypothesis rather than dogma.

### A Priori *Causality and Hegelian Causality*

The philosophic Marxists reject direct causality, first, because it is considered too determinist and "positivist"; it violates their acceptance of voluntarism, their assumption that people are free, undetermined, and capable of transforming the world at will (Pozzuto, 1973:54). Second, they reject direct causality because it is associated with an empiricist view of the world wherein relationships between variables can be observed objectively and stated straightforwardly; for the philosophics, reality is subjective, and direct objective observation is impossible. Third, the philosophics focus on the totality, not the parts. The generally accepted view of causality emphasizes the parts and their interrelations rather than the whole.

Some of the philosophic Marxists accept a form of explanation that could be characterized as a Hegelian type of causality: the whole unilaterally influences and determines the parts. As explained in Chapter 2, the totality expresses a "historical essence" such as capitalism, which influences all the elements of the totality. But this "Hegelian causality" is different from and contradictory to the generally accepted view of causality. It is unspecific about which changes in the whole cause particular changes in the parts: within Hegelian causality, the impact of the whole on the parts remains an amorphous process, vague and undefined.

The deductivists, much like the philosophics, reject any form of simple direct causality. It leaves no place for their fatalism/voluntarism, or their emphasis on the totality. They argue that cause and effect cannot be separated because of constant interaction, reciprocal dependence, and the "all-sidedness" of phenomena. Isolating causal relations from the "entire system of complex objective relations and the disregard of all other conditions cannot but distort the integral picture of the world" (Naletov, 1984:445). The "all-embracing character of the interaction of the world . . . is only one-sidedly, fragmentarily and incompletely expressed by causality" (Lenin, 1972:159). Although the deductivists would deny it, they impose an *a priori* form of causality on reality when they move beyond causality as a form of explanation to discuss the content of causal relations. They argue that the material, economic base or infrastructure causes the superstructure (social institutions) to be as it is because Marx said it was so. The content of this causality is quite distinct from that central to contemporary social science, and so it does not draw the deductivists any nearer to producing research that would be of interest to non-Marxists.

Neither the philosophics nor the deductivists accept the causal explanatory forms of contemporary social science within their respective sets of assumptions about inquiry. The Hegelian causality of the philosophics is not testable, not definite enough to permit the prediction and control which is the goal of causality within contemporary social science. The *a priori* causality of the deductivists is taken on faith, and the necessity to test such propositions is completely neglected.

### Structural Causality

The structuralists argue against direct causality as an explanatory form. First, their anti-empiricism leads them to object to direct causality because it requires quantifiable evidence. Second, direct causality focuses on the importance of the parts rather than the whole. The structuralists criticize this because it would require them to look at individual subjects and their actions, at events, and at the concrete historical origins of phenomena (Althusser and Balibar, 1968:164). They believe that a focus on these aspects of concrete reality is incompatible with their own commitment to understanding the world and change (what they call rupture) in terms of structures and higher level structural processes (Lecourt, 1975:15). They complain that direct causality leaves no room for understanding the depersonalized structural forces that work almost unconsciously, certainly without volition, but that wield their influence just the same at the structural level.

The structuralists are not opposed to causality in an absolute sense, "but it never acquires cogent centrality" in their analysis (Anderson, 1984:50). Certain aspects of their epistemological views are consistent with causality: acceptance of structural determinism, emphasis on the interaction of the totality and the parts, agreement with certain aspects of positivism, and claims of objectivity for their own research. So it is not surprising that many of the structuralists seek to redefine causality in terms that are more acceptable to their own analysis as a form of structural causality.

What is structural causality? How do the structuralists define it? Structural causality is multidimensional, a form of complex causality (Seung, 1982:113), a system of "intricate causal chains of 'mediation' and reciprocal effect" rather than direct unidimensional cause-and-effect relations (Therborn, 1976:10). This does not preclude a form of internal self-determination of structures wherein one substructure may be temporarily predominant at a particular moment. Reality is a "system of internal relations which is in the process of being structured through the operations of its own transformation rules." Research has to be "directed to discovering the transformation rules whereby society is constantly being restructured, rather than to finding 'causes' " (Harvey, 1973:289–90).

Although the structuralists do not reject causality itself, their view of it departs from that of contemporary social science. They use causal language, speaking of "necessary conditions and sufficient conditions," admittedly in rather imprecise terms. These Marxists attempt to examine how structures (which are invisible) arise and in turn give rise to change. They maintain that structural causality is objective and scientific. But the problem with this structural causality is that it is not open to being tested against reality. In addition, structural causality does not specify what exactly determines or causes a specific phenomenon; indeed, it would be impossible to do so because "a structure exists only in its effects and is not entirely present in any one of them." Although the structuralists point to the rate and timing of development of specific structures, they avoid direct causal statements. Precise prediction is also impossible because structures are constantly "combining, dissolving, and recombining." Everything is intimately linked to everything else at the level of structures. Feedback occurs immediately. A cause is "imminent in, not exterior to its effects" (Gorman, 1982:147–48; Althusser and Balibar, 1968:188–89). This precludes being very specific about causal links at any level or in terms of any unit of analysis. The structuralist's view of causality is so general and amorphous that it is not likely to produce theoretical statements that can be used to predict and provide a basis for intervention. In effect, structural causality redefines causality, transforming it into a form of inquiry, certainly not without interest but useful only for post hoc rationalization.

### Dialectics

Statements of a dialectical form are seldom found in contemporary non-Marxist research, but this form of explanation is central to Marxism. Does this mean that Marxist research is automatically jeopardized by its reference to the dialectic? Not exactly. Much depends on how the various Marxist groups define the dialectic, on how they relate it to causality, on how they use it to explain phenomena, and on the research role they attribute to it.

*The philosophics, structuralists, and deductivists hold views of the dialectic that are at odds with contemporary social science and unlikely to produce theories of value in policymaking.* The deductivists' version of the dialectic (dialectical materialism) denies the importance of direct causality and formal logic in general. The philosophics define the dialectic as all-encompassing and abstract, which is also inconsistent with direct causality. They emphasize dialectical and teleological explanation as an alternative to causal statements. The structuralists' response to dialectical explanation is mixed. Some reject it, whereas others try to reconcile it with structuralism. But the intention of nearly all of the structuralists is to move Marxism away from direct causality and the analysis of events and individuals toward a higher and more abstract focus, be it in the form of dialectics or structural causality.

*Although some materialist Marxists reject the dialectic and others ignore it, a third group defines it in a way that allows it to make a contribution to improving overall research strategy, of potential interest to Marxists and non-Marxists alike.* By itself the dialectic cannot provide policy-relevant explanation, but, as certain materialists have shown, it is not inherently incompatible with causality and can be useful in inquiry.

### The Deductivist Marxists: Dialectical Materialism

For the deductivist Marxists, the dialectic is expressed as dialectical materialism. The deductivists base their understanding of it on Stalin's interpretation of the writings of Lenin and Engels. The result is a form of the dialectic that is at once reductionist, abstract, and Hegelian. For the deductivists, dialectical materialism is all encompassing: a formal comprehensive logic, a set of laws, a universal system of thought, and a global, general method. It is said to apply to both the social and natural sciences, to nature and humankind. People are part of nature and are not of a special character apart from nature.

The deductivist Marxists' dialectical materialism is metaphysical rather than concrete. The world is not a complex of things but of processes. Matter takes an infinite diversity of forms that arise one from another and pass one into another. Things exist not as separate individual units but in essential relation and interconnection in a dynamic process.

Some of the deductivists conceive of dialectical materialism as a set of immutable, dogmatic rules or laws that describe and explain phenomena. First, small incremental changes give rise to large revolutionary ruptures (transformation of quantity into quality and vice versa). Second, reality is constituted of opposites which, although they appear in contradiction and conflict, are actually closely linked (unity of opposites or interpenetration of opposites). Third, when opposites clash, one eliminates the other but is, in turn, eliminated later at a higher level, so that there is an ongoing process of thesis, antithesis, and synthesis (negation of the negation). Stalin reformulated these laws and presented them in popular language, oversimplifying them and at the same time making them abstract.

Dialectical materialism also includes a special logic, dialectical logic, which is derived from the dialectical laws. The deductivists offer it as an alternative to formal logic because formal logic is said to be flawed through its association with capitalism and its inability to take into account the contradictory character of reality.

The deductivists' view of dialectics as an explanatory form is incompatible with contemporary social science. If everything is interacting with everything else, this constitutes a multiple feedback system, a situation where it is mathematically and logically impossible to state the implications of any specific change in the system. There is no room for direct causality; even the useful aspects of positivism are rejected as is apparent in the defense of the dialectic by the Soviet deductivist Igor Naletov (1984). The dialectic is presented as an alternative explanatory form that is assumed, *a priori*, to apply to the whole range of phenomena. Empirical research is rejected. Dialectical logic denies the validity of formal logic. The deductivists' view of the dialectic simply rules out two of the primary pillars of modern science, namely, formal logic and causal statements, with a corresponding impact on the value of their research efforts for non-Marxists.

### Philosophic Marxists: Idealist Dialectics and Teleology

Philosophic Marxists reject direct causality as a form of explanation, but they retain dialectics and teleology, making both central to their own method. By teleology they mean that the effect precedes the cause and determines it. A preconceived state of affairs, or a goal, acts as a cause of human activity, even though it would appear to an observer as an effect. Within this form of explanation, "the relationship between cause and effect is overturned" (Pozzuto, 1973:53–54). Direct causality breaks down because the effect is a preconceived state of affairs. For the philosophics, teleology implies purposeful action toward a goal. Conscious human intent becomes a motivating force. It exists prior to action and is simultaneously the end result of action. But teleology is more than merely motivational. For some of the philosophics, it is metaphysical as well, implying anything that happens was predestined beforehand; there is a grand design in the "nature of things."

The philosophics strongly object to the way other Marxist groups define the dialectic. They criticize the deductivists' view that the dialectic is a rigorously structured logic or a set of laws. This does not mean that they accept non-Marxist formal logic which they say "supports the *status quo*" and is associated with capitalism, its division of labor, and reification. They also criticize the deductivist's dialectic as simplistic and mechanical. The philosophic's own version of the dialectic is Hegelian in character, highly theoretical and abstract in form, and idealist in content. They see it as a universal explanatory form that includes a metaphysical, ontological understanding of the universe, a method of knowing, a means to awareness, and a will to transform society (Lefebvre, 1969a:103). Most importantly, it is a "description of the process of movement in the world" (Thomas, 1977:51). The dialectic applies only to history and society, never to nature. If it applied to both equally, they say, people would be assumed to be part of nature rather than qualitatively different from all other forms of life.

The philosophics understand dialectics as an alternative to direct causality. Within dialectical explanation "every cause of an effect can be considered at the same time an effect of an effect." Instantaneous reciprocal influence is the rule. The effect of one element on another element is like an "incorporation, a reflection, a manifestation of the dominant process in the other." The mechanisms of this developmental process are internal. They may be asymmetrical, but the "relatively less influential force immediately contributes back on the shaping of the character of its reciprocal" (Karmen, 1972:24–27). Conflict and contradiction propel phenomena forward. The tension inherent in the polarity of opposites will disappear only after the revolution when opposites will be resolved and overcome (Lukacs, 1971). The dialectic is not an objective explanatory form, but rather an expression of the "subjective lawfulness of men" (Breines, 1972:82).

From the point of view of systematic research, the philosophics' abstract mystical, metaphysical, Hegelian dialectic presents many of the same problems as those posed by the deductivists' equally idealist dialectic (Palmer, 1981:46). It is not, and cannot be, constrained by reality. It is assumed to be a viable alternative to rigorous observation and scientific inquiry. Systematic study is impossible because everything is in a constant state of flux, changing from one moment to the next. Conclusions based on the dialectic, as formulated by the philosophics, are far too subjective to be of interest to non-Marxists who agree with the generally accepted model of contemporary social science inquiry.

Certain philosophics refer to their dialectic as "concrete" (Kosik, 1976), which can be very misleading. They do not mean empirical-concrete. Rather, they use the term "concrete" to refer to the "view of a self-contained totality," the "subject-object identity," and the process of "synthesizing contradictions" (Sekine, 1980). Even though such Marxists call their view of the dialectic "concrete," the content they attribute to the dialectic is identical with that of the other philosophics, and the implications for research are the same.

### Structuralist Marxists: Optional Dialectics

The structuralists deny the utility of the kind of direct, individual-level, causal explanatory forms that are essential to modern social science. They propose an alternative form—structural causality. What, then, is the role of dialectical explanation for the structuralists? There is considerable variation within the group.

Some of the structuralists argue that dialectical laws constitute a useful explanatory form. They contend that neither direct causal explanation nor dialectical explanation aiming at general global laws governing society (as the philosophics and deductivists propose) can substitute for structural causality (Harvey, 1973:287).

Another group of structuralists retains dialectical explanation. They define it in terms of structuralist configurations rather than as confrontations between individuals or specific concrete institutions. Some of the structuralists demonstrate considerable intellectual agility in reconciling dialectical laws to structuralist concepts. Thus, the transformation of quantity into quality is related to what they call "rupture"; the identity of opposites is linked to primary and secondary contradiction; the principle of negation of the negation is interpreted in terms of the process of overdetermination (Meunier, 1973). Althusser's concept of overdetermination has also been understood as a form of dialectical structure which assumes, all at once, relative autonomy and reciprocal determination, relative dependence and relative independence (Seung, 1982:114–15).

Dialectical laws are neither essential to structuralist Marxism nor incompatible with it. But no matter how well these Marxists harmonize structuralist causality and dialectics, they still do not satisfy the methodological requirements of contemporary scientific inquiry. Their use of the dialectic remains vague, resting on "theoretical work" rather than on concrete research to identify structures. Specific predictions are not considered important.

### Materialist Marxists and the Dialectic

Materialist Marxists manifest a number of different reactions to the dialectic as an explanatory form. One group rejects it entirely, a second group simply ignores it, and a third retains it but without special or sacrosanct status, attempting to define it in a way that does not preclude direct causality and is therefore consistent with rigorous defensible research. Almost all of the materialists reject the view that the dialectic offers a special type of logic that supersedes formal logic. For them, formal logic corresponds to events in the real world, even if certain exceptions to it arise from time to time. They also reject the dialectic as a set of laws.

The first group of materialists, which rejects the dialectic entirely, labels it idealistic and unscientific. Historically, some of the Austro-Marxists (not Adler) and certain members of the Second International found the dialectic so abstract, and so often abused, that they dismissed it altogether, considering it nonessential to their Marxism and their research. Nikolai Bukharin rejected dialectics, arguing that it was inappropriate under post-revolutionary socialism in the USSR. Edward Bernstein and other members of the Second International also accorded little value to it. Traditionally, the materialists have attributed greater importance to direct causality than have other Marxists. More recently, certain materialists have discarded the dialectic in an attempt to mark the distance between themselves and both the philosophic Marxists in the West and the deductivist Marxists in the socialist countries.

The second group of materialists, which ignores the dialectic, argues that Marx himself never explained anything by the laws of dialectics, although on occasion he did not avoid "the dialectical vocabulary of obscurantism" (Mills, 1962:129). They also point out that very little that is said with "dialectical language" cannot be said more directly and straightforwardly with ordinary language.

The third group of materialists conserves the dialectic as an explanatory form that focuses on real objects and reminds us "not to lose them utterly in idealized abstractions" (Lewontin and Levins, 1976:60). They attempt to reconcile the dialectic with empirical social science, to understand it as a research tool, to make it more concrete, and to subject the results it produces to testing. At the same time, most of these Marxists preserve causal explanation as complementary to dialectical explanation. These materialists are unwilling to assume either that the dialectic applies only to social phenomena or that it is equally applicable to both nature and society. They argue that its appropriateness must be determined on the basis of investigation rather than in an *a priori* fashion.

Some of the efforts of this third group to salvage the dialectic are worth closer scrutiny. One of their proposals is to synthesize the dialectic and the generally accepted model of research. Johan Galtung, for example, argues that the distinction between Western social science and dialectics is "not that sharp, the dichotomy not that absolute; constructing from some of the tools used in positivist methodology, a methodology compatible with dialectic insight should not be impossible." Galtung describes positivism as technique without understanding and dialectics as understanding that has not been made operational. Although they are at the opposite ends of a continuum, a reevaluation of each could be made allowing them to coexist and complement each other (Galtung, 1977:214–15, 228–29).

Another effort by a materialist Marxist to save the dialectic without abandoning causal explanation interprets Marx's dialectic concretely, not as a finished system of thought but rather as having empirical content (Sherman, 1976). The goal is to transform the dialectic into a legitimate scientific operation or an "empirically based methodology" (Allen, 1975:206). These Marxists argue that in some situations direct causality corresponds to reality, but in other situations dialectical explanation may be more appropriate. In fact, because of the way these materialists conceive of the dialectic, as concrete rather than abstract, it is often difficult to distinguish it from causal explanation.

This third group of materialists describes the dialectic so that it is of considerable value to Marxists and non-Marxists alike. It adds to one's strategy of inquiry by encouraging an awareness of the broad range of theoretical contexts possible. In this form the dialectic is formulated as a series of questions or hypotheses which the researcher presents with respect to a specific data set. It provides useful instructions for inquiry because it reminds the researcher that things are evolving, that change may be the result of internal forces rather than exclusively external, that dramatic transformation may result from prior small quantitative changes, that phenomena occur in contexts and are not completely detached from the rest of the world.

In what direction does this type of materialist dialectic point us in terms of methodology? First, it does not assume that the subject matter of inquiry is static prior to investigation. It encourages one to look for change and evolution in what is being studied. Second, when a change is observed, it suggests that it may be the result of forces internal to what is being studied, appropriately conceived as a struggle between opposite elements. An effort should be made to locate these "interpenetrating, contending opposing elements and forces" to discover what is the nature of the conflict, the direction it is taking, and, in a conflict of opposing forces, which one is stronger (Somerville, 1967:70). When one aspect of a phenomenon appears to be completely eliminated, the researcher should ask if the new entity resulting from conflict may also contain within itself the roots of its own destruction or transformation. How does the new supersede the old? Third, when what is being studied is marked by a dramatic transformation, the materialist dialectic suggests that small quantitative changes may have been responsible. Finally, researchers are encouraged to take a relational point of view, looking for interactions rather than treating phenomena in isolation. This implies inserting data into context and interpreting them from a situational perspective rather than singularly and as independent phenomena (Lewontin and Levins, 1976:60).

The materialist dialectic also focuses on the historical aspect of reality and evolutionary development. It asks the following questions: "Where has this subject matter come from, and where is it going? What were the circumstances of the origin of its present form? What are the main lines along which it is now changing, in regard to concrete content and rate?" (Somerville, 1967:70). The materialist dialectic reminds us "to formulate the regularities and trends found in the world as specific to a particular historical epoch," and it "cautions us not to generalize beyond the confines of this epoch" (Mills, 1962).

No one can say in advance whether or not the openings in research strategy proposed by the materialists' understanding of the dialectic will be fruitful, but they are of potential interest to non-Marxists. In this form the dialectic encourages one to put a small set into a larger structure, to be aware of a variety of contexts, to put a specific time within a larger time frame, not to get too caught up with too long a time span because there may be a break in the observed pattern, and to watch for modifications in the rate of change without external input. In this form the dialectic could possibly add to the strategy of inquiry which one takes into research. Although in its presentation it is limited to post hoc formulations, if employed in research it could even contribute to the production of better causal theories and a more adequate basis for action.

### Explanatory Forms: Summary

Marxists use three explanatory forms: dialectics, causality, and teleology. We have seen that teleology is unlikely to be of use in producing defensible theory in terms of the generally accepted model. The dialectic, if it is to be of value, must be defined so that it is compatible with, or supplementary to, causality, and not as a substitute for causal explanation. The rules or statements of a theory must be constrained by reality (testable) and causal in form, especially if they are to be of use in policymaking; without this requirement, intervention to produce or inhibit events is impossible.

A summary of the whole section on explanatory forms illustrates the variety of methodological positions taken by the various branches of contemporary Marxism with respect to the character of the rules that constitute theories. The philosophics discard direct causal explanation, approve a form of "Hegelian causality," but argue most enthusiastically for what they offer as a substitute for direct causality, that is, their Hegelian version of dialectics or teleological explanation. The deductivists reject direct causality and support a version of dialectical materialism as a universal explanatory form that can be understood as a form of *a priori* causality. The structuralists are opposed to direct causality but have a mixed response to the dialectic. Some try to reconcile structuralism to dialectical explanation; others emphasize structural causality but not in a form recognized by contemporary social science. Some of the materialists reject the dialectic, others ignore it, and still others define it concretely, so that it can be of use in improving overall research strategy. Those who define it concretely consider the dialectic to complement causal explanations. Only the materialists retain direct causal explanation as understood in the generally accepted model of research outlined in Chaper 1. The efforts of the other Marxists to redefine causality, by whatever term ("Hegelian," *a priori*, or "structural"), do not alter this conclusion. Their modified versions of causality are of little use in producing theories acceptable within contemporary social science or of value in policymaking. No further reference will be made to these forms of causality. Henceforth, causality refers strictly to direct causality.

## THEORY: CONSTRUCTION, TESTING, AND APPLICATION

According to the generally accepted model of social science, theory is a set of related statements, generalizations, and/or explanations that can be tested. Each theory is tentative and conditional, never "true" in the formal or absolute sense. This definition is insufficient, however, for those seeking theory that can be used for intervention. If policymaking is the goal, theory is more profitably viewed as a a set of rule-like statements linking concepts or variables in a causal manner under certain specified conditions. Such theories provide grounds for action intended to produce known consequences (Meehan, 1982:84, 118). While not dismissing the more general conception of theory, the policymaking model will be emphasized here because it is the more demanding of the two, and the limiting conditions governing production and use are the same in both cases.

This section focuses on the methodologically relevant aspects of theory: its construction, its testing, and its application. From the perspective of the policymaking model, theory application is a way of testing theory. (The other ways are to test it against history and against established knowledge.) But application in terms of this model involves something more, namely, the use of theory for the achievement of purposes. Some Marxists also attribute special significance to application, defining it with respect to practice or praxis. For all these reasons application will be treated separately below.

The epistemological and methodological assumptions of the various Marxist orientations influence how they construct, test, and apply theory. These matters in turn influence how Marxists do research (Chapter 5), how they defend their knowledge claims, and how they merge the normative and the empirical to construct policy (Chapter 6).

In our exploration of Marxist views of theory here, we will see that only the materialists seem to have the potential to produce theory that is of interest within the context of either the generally accepted model or the policymaking model. This is because only they among the Marxists agree that theory should be (1) constructed on the basis of observation and data, (2) tested against concrete reality, (3) and applied in an additional effort to test it and obtain feedback. When they talk about practice, they mean the application of knowledge to the real world for testing and correction. Most of the structuralists see theory as exclusively intellectual in construction and subject to testing or evaluation only in terms of internal intellectual coherence. The philosophics attribute great importance to theory, but they construct and test it in subjective terms or on the basis of political priorities without reference to evidence. Neither the structuralists nor the philosophics define praxis or practice as a test of theory. The deductivists construct theory in an *a priori* manner, reasoning from their rather rigid interpretation of what Marx and his successors wrote. The only test of new theory that counts for them is how closely it conforms to the pre-given tenets. They do not consider practice to be a means of testing theory; rather, they see it as the application of historical materialism.

### Theory Construction

To be useful in dealing with real problems, theory needs to be constructed on the basis of observation or experience which makes reference to concrete reality. It involves interpretation (which is constrained by evidence) and concepts with indicators that refer to data and are defined (largely) in real terms. Such theories consist of rules that include causal explanatory forms, are testable in principle, and potentially can be applied in the real world. We will see that only some of the materialist Marxists accept a method of theory construction that meets these requirements.

For the philosophics theory is the result of reflection. It is constructed in the sense of being subjectively realized in thought. Most of these Marxists dismiss the value of data in theory-building, and their concepts are almost exclusively nominal. Because they reject the possibility of objectivity, observed experience is assumed to be misleading. They see theory as being dependent on subjective experience defined from an idealist (classical) point of view. The philosophics who emphasize the superiority of a working-class perspective insist that theory be constructed from the point of view of the proletariat, out of experience gained in the class struggle. Here too, experience is defined subjectively, dependent on introspection, intuition, and observation which are understood to be class-determined.

Theory, produced through abstraction, is also of primary importance to the structuralists because, as Althusser contends, it transforms ideology into knowledge. As he describes it, theory is itself a form of practice or activity in which the real world is appropriated by thought (Althusser and Balibar, 1968:55–59). By this he means that reality is simply seized or taken over by the mind. This conception has important consequences for theory construction. Theoretical practice, like any other practice, is defined as the "process of *transformation* of a determinate given raw material into a determinate product," undertaken by human labor "using determinate means of ('production')" (1965:166). Althusser means that theory, arrived at through intellectual abstraction, is, like any other activity, a form of work once removed from reality. It involves transforming a specific object into something more sophisticated in character, with the help of the tools available to do such labor at any particular point in time. What distinguishes theoretical practice from other practices is that it takes place entirely in the realm of thought (Althusser and Balibar, 1968:42). Theories, as defined by Althusser, generate their own explanations and predictions out of their own intellectual procedures, without reference to reality. According to Althusser, in the structuralists' view of theory construction there is no role for data, real concepts with indicators, observation of the real world, or empirical investigation in general. Not all of the structuralist Marxists agree with Althusser on this point, as will be explained in Chapter 5.

The way the deductivists construct theory departs markedly from the general practice of contemporary social science but for reasons quite different from those of the philosophics and structuralists. The deductivists see theory (in terms of historical materialism) as a general, objective, final and complete, scientific explanation (Szczepanski, 1966:48). They reject the view that their own theory is tentative, conditional, or potentially subject to refinement. They assume that their theory, historical materialism, applies to all phenomena, for all time; it is at once universal and eternal. New theory is generated from what Marx and his successors wrote. The deductivists argue that theory is developed by postulation or deduction, prior to the creation of low-level hypotheses and therefore prior to observation or the generalization of the results of observation. The deductivists do not deny the role of observation in the *initial* construction and formulation of the theory. Indeed, they contend that Marx made careful observations in the process of historical materialism. But they question the need for further observations before formulating new theory because this would mean Marx's work was incomplete. As the deductivists see it, if theory construction is guided by Marx's writings, truth is assured. Data are no longer required because that process was completed, for the most part, by Marx. Data and observable experience are used only to illustrate the correctness of the theory (Lektorsky and Melyukhin, 1977:84).

The materialist Marxists agree among themselves on the importance of data, of concepts defined in real terms, and of observation in theory construction. They argue with each other on how far this commitment to theory construction should go in challenging the hegemony of that theory which constitutes the Marxian heritage. But there is a consensus among them that Marx did not complete theory construction for all time.

Many materialists, especially those in the socialist countries, advance the different-levels view of theory which opens historical materialism to modification but does not really challenge its basic character. These Marxists begin by conceding to historical materialism the role of providing the most general laws of nature, society, and thought. They concentrate on theory construction at a lower level, and the independent, non-competing "special theories" they produce in specific fields may be of interest to non-Marxists. In return for the concessions these Marxists make to historical materialism, often strategically motivated, special disciplines are recognized to be entitled to independent points of view on specific problems (Kamenka, 1969). Historical materialism still serves as a methodological foundation for their social research, but greater freedom exists in terms of concepts, methods, and, by implication, research organizational support structures.

Other materialists define the role of research in theory construction as that of enlarging and transforming the general principles of historical materialism which they say is scientific (based on evidence) and designed to be tested with empirical evidence, now and in the future. For these Marxists historical materialism was never meant to be more than a provisional statement, to be refined and improved as new evidence became available and new phenomena appeared which Marx could not have foreseen. These Marxists set out to test and reconstruct Marx's theory, to indicate which parts of it remain valid, which need to be refined, and which must be thrown out entirely. Data and observation provide information for updating historical materialism. Rigorous research becomes "an 'empirical arm,' a set of technical tools and procedural devices designed to supply theoreticians with facts for further generalizations" (Shalin, 1978:177).

Finally, some materialist Marxists believe that rigorous research and theory development require complete autonomy from historical materialism, which is viewed as merely an historically specific theory of the origins and evolution of capitalism. Theory construction, they say, must go beyond just developing Marx's ideas or perfecting them or even testing them, to constructing new theory that does not necessarily coincide with historical materialism (Szczepanski, 1966:48, 51).

The materialists see theory construction as based on data and observation, a view that does not diverge much from that of contemporary social science. This is not the case for the other Marxists. The philosophics construct theory out of reflection and subjective experience, sometimes of a political character. The structuralists, thanks to Althusser, see it as exclusively abstraction, intellectual work. For the deductivists it involves reasoning from historical materialism to new topics.

## Testing Theory

A theory cannot be proved or disproved for all time, but its adequacy can be evaluated. Theory can be judged on whether or not it is consistent with already existing theories to determine if it holds in light of what is already known. It can also be evaluated with respect to its internal characteristics (coherence, aesthetic qualities, range and depth of explanation, consistency, and logic). Finally, it can be tested, at least in principle, to ascertain whether the evidence supporting it outweighs that which calls it into question.

Although testing with any number of forms of evidence is considered sufficient for the generally accepted model of social science research, the policymaking model requires more. Theories that aim to provide the basis of action must be testable in the sense that the "relations specified in the rules of the theory must fit the events of the real world" (Meehan, 1982:107). In other words, theories must work. In the case of this policymaking model, theory must be tested with respect to purpose, and observation must tell whether or not the chosen outcome is achieved.

We will first consider how Marxists view forms of evidence, and, then examine evidence from theory application in the following section. In terms acceptable to contemporary social science, evidence can be understood to include empirically observable experience, observation of the historical record, laboratory experiments, results of formal social science research and information acquired in application (measured outcomes of implementation or use of theories in policymaking situations). No matter what form of evidence is used, ultimately, if a test is a good one, the data must have primacy over the theory in the sense that theory has to conform to data rather than vice versa.

Not all Marxists test theory in ways acceptable to modern social science. The philosophics and the structuralists are immune to data requirements and show little concern for the necessity to test theory with evidence. The structuralists propose evaluating a theory on the basis of its internal characteristics. The philosophics argue that intuition, introspection, or political orientation are ample "evidence." The deductivists also reject testing theory against observable experience. Instead, they merely seek to assure consistency of theory with historical materialism, independently of data or observation. The materialists seek to test theories much as do non-Marxist social scientists, marshalling relevant evidence in a variety of forms as required by the generally accepted model.

The philosophic Marxists do not seek to evaluate the adequacy of their theories against evidence or by comparison with reality. They advise against the use of data or observation to test theory. As noted above, they say that data are produced by the researcher and amount to little more than mere inventions of the creative human mind. Observation, distorted under capitalism, can be of no help. As a substitute for evaluating theories against evidence, the philosophics argue for judging it on the basis of intuition and introspection derived from one's daily life experience. Many of them reject the possibility of predictive theory, maintaining that it is a logical impossibility in a world where conscious humans are free to determine their own lives because the unexpected can break through at any time (Van Steenbergen, 1970:95).

Those philosophics who argue that theory originates and is constructed on the basis of experience gained in political action also reject most data and most observed experience as tests of theory. However, they do suggest that evidence for testing theory can be gained by analyzing history and in the act of class struggle. Such forms of evidence are considered objective because they are expressions of the working-class perspective and, as we saw before with respect to other aspects of their epistemology and methodology, are assumed to be superior to other points of view. But, in the end, the adequacy of their theories is not judged on the basis of this type of evidence. They have a more important criterion for evaluating theory, whether or not it serves the interest of the proletariat. Evidence is not excluded, but it plays a secondary role in relation to political goals.

Althusser and the structuralists reject contemporary social science norms regarding the testing of theory. This view follows logically from their understanding of theory construction as "theoretical practice," as an intellectual process. They deny the need to test theory against evidence. Althusser rejects "actual empirical engagements with social reality" (E. P. Thompson, 1978:124). As they see it, data are products of the theory in which they are constructed (Burris, 1979b:9). Because each individual has his or her reading of reality, there is no basis in external evidence for judging any particular theory's adequacy (Appelbaum, 1979:23). Althusser argues that to require such testing is merely pragmatism, which he rejects. No true science, he observes, ever depends on such outside verification (Althusser and Balibar, 1968:59; Althusser, 1965:173). Because only abstract structures are authentic and they cannot be directly observed, there is no reason to try to compare them with the "data of the social world."

Althusser is especially hostile to history as a source of evidence for testing theory. His objections refer to the underlying assumptions of history itself which he says imply a view of time as read on a calendar, as continuous. He argues that time is complex and non-linear. Structures have different, independent time sequences and do not coexist in the same time frame. He objects to the empiricism implicit within a historical perspective, constituted of a succession of events. He maintains that little can be learned from history about what is going on at the moment. He attributes primacy to the present over the past (Althusser and Balibar, 1968:61–63, 125).

As an alternative to the testing of theory, Althusser suggests that it should be evaluated on the basis of its internal characteristics. Theory "depends on the internal articulation and development of its discourse, not upon the pseudo-innocence of an appeal to experience or experiment" (Blackburn and Jones, 1972:376). Althusser reasons that theory produces a special object (knowledge) which has its own internal criteria of validity. There are, he continues, "definite protocols with which to *validate* the quality of its product [theory], i.e., the criteria of the scientificity of the products of scientific practice" (Althusser and Balibar, 1968:59). While vague on the specifics, Althusser seems to argue that theory should be evaluated by strictly logical, intellectual procedures. The adequacy of a theory rests entirely with the beauty of the theoretical structure, the systematization of its concepts, its analytical rigor, its *internal* consistency, and its logic (Althusser, 1977:9; Therborn, 1976:42). None of these criteria is without importance. But the question remains. Are they sufficient? Can a theory be of value in and of itself, independently of concrete reality? Without testing the adequacy of a theory by comparison with reality, there is little possibility of correcting mistakes internal to the theoretical structures. Theory tested only with respect to internal criteria cannot produce knowledge useful for policymaking because it is designed to be of use, not in changing reality, but only in describing it abstractly.

The deductivists do not test their theories as required by the generally accepted model. Testing in the normal sense of the word is meaningless to them. It does not enter into the process of testing theory as they conceive of it because historical materialism is understood to be a finished, theoretical structure that cannot be amended without threatening "the integrity of the whole" (Szczepanski, 1966:48–49). It is subject to its own special form of testing (Lektorsky and Melyukhin, 1977:81–84). In short, because the Bolsheviks' revolution in 1917 overthrew the state and the bourgeoisie, historical materialism is said to have been tested and its validity established for all time. Any new theory is adequate only if it "is obtained with the methodological guidance of historical materialism" (Lysmankin, 1977:213). As we saw earlier in this chapter, the deductivists attribute little value to data and observation. It is hardly surprising, then, that they consider them of secondary importance in testing theory.

Some of the materialist Marxists hold that "special theories" must be testable (in principle) with evidence; other materialists extend the requirement to historical materialism itself. Whatever the case, *the materialists agree that if theories do not correspond to reality, if they are inconsistent with evidence grounded in data and observation, they must be abandoned* (McQuarie, 1976:217). The materialists define evidence in broad terms to include historical experience, research results, experiments, and information gained from application. It is to application that we now turn.

In sum, the philosophics test theory on the basis of personal or political experience. The structuralists evaluate it according to the logic of its internal characteristics; and the deductivists test theory by comparing it to a set of pre-given tenets. The materialists test it against data and observation, more or less as required by the norms of modern social science.

### Theory Application and Practice

For some Marxists the application of theory is best understood in relation to what they call practice or praxis. These terms are important defining characteristics of Marxism, setting it off from non-Marxist views of the world. Practice/praxis refers, on the broadest level, to intervention or activity in the real world. In the case of the materialists, practice contributes to their research strategy and improves their theories in terms recognized by contemporary social science.

For materialist Marxists, practice, ranging from class struggle to laboratory experiments, includes the application of theory to real world conditions. Policy implementation in this context is structured to constitute a test of theory. The goal of applying theory in the process of practice is to refine and correct it, to improve its predictability, and to detect if "it can achieve the objectives one has in mind" (Mao Zedong, 1966:14). Otto Neurath, along with many materialists in the Second International, argued that social research is to the socialist state planning system as laboratory experiments are to the natural sciences (Bottomore, 1983:383).

As a consequence of introducing practice as an integral part of method, the materialists retain contact with reality through their research. It keeps them in touch with contemporary social science and prevents their theories from becoming too abstract to be of any use. The materialists' view of practice as theory application is partly linked to their epistemological and methodological orientation. But it is also a result of their familiarity with the problems of real world decision-making. Marxists of this orientation have often held political office in various countries. Through this experience at least some of them have come to understand the need to orient theory toward the practical and to make it useful in administration. It is not surprising that they insist on evaluating theory on the basis of whether or not it works.

The deductivists seldom apply their theories to obtain feedback, to refine it, and to correct it. Like the materialists, the deductivists have held power in various countries during the twentieth century, but this has not increased their interest in testing their theory with evidence. They reverse the relation between theory construction and testing. As they define it, practice does not refer to testing theory in the real world; rather, it means applying historical materialism to reality in order to create the concrete situation deemed desirable by the theory or by the party's interpretation of the theory. Practice for them means self-confirmation. The application of theory serves to illustrate its correctness, to demonstrate its predictive capacity rather than to test it.

The implications of the deductivists' conception of theory application for research are serious. Theories that do not challenge historical materialism are accepted without question. In addition, the deductivists sometimes reject theory that is sustained by objective evidence because it appears to contradict historical materialism. In the past, when in power, the deductivists have sacrificed production, economic development and efficiency, and human lives to maintain consistency with their theoretical choice, that is, historical materialism. Numerous examples of this occurred in China during the years of the Cultural Revolution. For example, because theory dictated the harmony of intellectual and manual labor, scientists and technicians with the skills required for modernization were sent to the countryside where they were assigned tasks far below their abilities.

Deductivists seem to believe that they serve "the party by violating experience, by overlooking embarrassing details, by grossly simplifying the data" (Sartre, 1963:20–30). Such practices encourage self-deception; ultimately, the ability to distinguish between objective reality and what one would like the world to be simply disappears. The unpleasant aspects of reality are ignored only at a cost, for reality cannot be suppressed indefinitely, however strong one's beliefs. When practice ceases to be a means of testing and becomes a means of preserving the regime, it is no longer compatible with the requirement of contemporary research that research findings be testable and tested, that the results of application be used to refine theory.

The philosophics reject the materialists' view of practice. They prefer the word "praxis" to practice, defining it as humanist creativity, individual emancipation, and intellectual human development. Praxis refers to the act by which men and women change the world and themselves. By praxis the philosophics do not mean testing theory through application in the real world.

The structuralists also discuss theory as praxis or practice. Althusser states that there are four kinds of production and four practices that go along with them: material, political, cultural, and theoretical. But he limits the potential of practice to "intervention" in the realm of the theoretical (Althusser, 1971:61). Arguing against the materialists, he says that practice must not be reduced to experimentation or application, "for to do so would be to separate it from intellectual activity" (Wetter, 1964:11). As Althusser puts it, philosophy is practice, and intellectual theorizing constitutes "class struggle in the field of theory" (Althusser, 1972:311). This leads him to a dubious conclusion: "It has been possible to apply Marx's theory with success because it is 'true'; it is not true because it has been applied with success" (Althusser and Balibar, 1968:59).

In sum, although practice/praxis is a special preoccupation of Marxists, whether or not it is useful in the sense of testing theory depends on how it is defined. The materialists understand practice to include the application of theory to real world events; hence, it constitutes a means to test and improve theory. For the deductivists, it means the application of historical materialism to reality; for the philosophics it is never used in the research-relevant sense but rather refers to human development. The structuralists reject practice as application of theory and instead limit it to the realm of thought.

### Theory: Conclusion

The materialist Marxists adopt methodological principles relating to theory, which would be considered acceptable within the framework of contemporary social science, that is, constructed on the basis of data and observation, incorporating concepts defined in real terms, and testable in principle by reference to evidence in the real world. They apply theory in what they call the "process of practice," so that application is viewed as testing theory in line with the policymaking model. This is true even of those materialists who advocate the different-levels view of theory construction. Their concessions to historical materialism constitute an important limitation, but they matter less in cases where theory construction pertains to "lower level" subjects considered to have a certain independence from the more general level historical materialism.

Dogmatism marks the deductivists' view of the construction, testing, and application of theory because they require that data and observation conform to predetermined theory. Objectivity is sacrificed in order to protect the integrity of the theory. The writings of Marx and Lenin precede and dictate the character of evidence used to support theory. The views of the founders function as a rigid framework for description, categorization, and classification. New theory, which is evaluated in terms of its consistency with Marx, Lenin, and so on, rather than in empirical terms, is expected to create the concrete reality desired by the Communist Party. As a result, theorizing amounts to little more than an effort to "prove" and "demonstrate" what is already accepted. The content of theory and the method of construction and testing theory are fused. "The fundamentals of scientific theory are simultaneously the methodological principles of scientific analysis" (Ukraintsev, 1978:91). The methodology is assumed to guarantee the ability to predict outcomes and control the environment, a judgment which is hardly likely to be convincing to non-Marxists or Marxists of a different orientation.

The philosophics see theory construction in idealist terms, as a reflective, subjective process. Testing is meaningless within the context of their epistemological and methodological assumptions. For them, theory means evaluation on the basis of intuition, introspection, or political criteria.

The structuralists, like the philosophics, reject any role for data and observation in theory construction or testing. For these Marxists theory is a product of intellectual work, abstraction, and is to be judged solely on the basis of its internal characteristics. Neither the philosophics nor the structuralists define practice/praxis so that it includes testing theory through application in the real world. Because they do not develop theory and test it by application, no corrective mechanisms are in place for improving future efforts. Given their methodological assumptions, these Marxists are unlikely to produce theory with any kind of predictive capacity or of use in terms of contemporary social science.

### RESEARCH IMPLICATIONS OF MARXIST METHODOLOGICAL ASSUMPTIONS: SUMMARY

In this chapter we have examined some of the methodological requirements that promote research in terms of the generally accepted model and that must be met if research is to contribute to the production of knowledge which can serve as a basis for action. The division among Marxists on these matters is substantial and far reaching in importance. The materialist Marxists were found to hold methodological assumptions that are fairly close to the requirements of contemporary social science. They alone among the Marxists choose methodological principles that are likely to promote research and to be accepted and usable by those non-Marxists who agree with the generally accepted model. Across the whole range of methodological questions they make choices that are constrained by reality, dependent on empirically grounded evidence.

The materialist Marxists give priority to induction rather than deduction; their research begins with the concrete rather than the abstract. Although they are aware of the problems involved in observation and the difficulty of going beyond appearances, they are optimistic about overcoming them. They acknowledge that there may be any number of valid, consistent interpretations. Data, however, refer to the real world, and contradictory sets of interpretations cannot stand. Given two conflicting interpretations, at least one and perhaps both are wrong. Many of their concepts are defined in real terms. They are preoccupied with linking concepts to measurable indicators. The materialist Marxists emphasize causal explanatory forms. Those among them who retain the dialectic define it concretely, so that it does not exclude causality and in some cases actually contributes to the formulation of a more sophisticated research strategy. They view theory as constructed on the basis of data and observation, involving real concepts, and tested as required by contemporary social science. They include a broad definition of what constitutes evidence for testing. The materialists understand practice to be the application of theory, one important form of testing, part of the ongoing process of correcting and refining theory.

The structuralist, deductivist, and philosophic Marxists choose an idealist point of departure for inquiry beginning with theory, with the abstract. They reject an inductive approach, and they are pessimistic about the value of observation which, they say, can only be superficial. Most of them consider interpretation to be an entirely subjective process unconstrained by reality. The philosophics view interpretation, defined as the process by which one constructs or creates reality, as central to their method of inquiry. Each of these groups minimizes the value of data for research. Their concepts are for the most part nominalist rather than real. They are not concerned with linking concepts to measurable indicators. None of these Marxists uses the kind of causal explanatory form considered valid within contemporary social science. The philosophics replace direct causality with "Hegelian causality." This abstract form of the dialectic and teleology are central to their method. The structuralists develop a form of "structural causality" which has little in common with direct causality. The deductivists substitute a rigid form of dialectical materialism for causal explanation. The philosophic and structuralist Marxists construct theory on the basis of exclusively intellectual or subjectivist grounds and see little value in testing theory with evidence or applying it in the real world. The deductivists maintain that the writings of Marx and his approved successors provide a sufficient base for constructing new theory. The only test they are willing to apply involves assuring that the new theory is consistent with the orthodox position. Application of theory amounts only to putting theory, historical materialism, into practice, not testing it. Prediction derives from theory alone, not from theory linked to observation. None of these Marxists attributes much of a role to observation or to data in the construction or testing of theory.

*The general methodological assumptions of the philosophic, structuralist, and deductivist Marxists, unlike those of the materialists, are independent of any empirical referent.* This influences how they undertake research (Chapter 5), how they defend their knowledge claims, and how they produce policy (Chapter 6). But before examining these matters we will first look at Marxist assumptions about science.

# 4.

# MARXIST VIEWS OF SCIENCE

Four dimensions of Marxist views on science, each of which influences how they do research, are discussed in this chapter. First, Marxist evaluations of modern science are explored. Second, how they define their own research with respect to science and whether or not their respective conceptions of science correspond to the requirements of the generally accepted model are considered. Third, how they understand the relationship between politics and science is examined. Fourth, how Marxists link class and science is presented.

This chapter is concerned not so much with the assumptions that underlie science as with the more general level assumptions which Marxists make about science and how they understand the scientific enterprise itself. Marxists are unlikely to produce defensible research in terms of the generally accepted model if they take any of the following positions concerning science: (1) repudiate modern science altogether, (2) reject any attempt to make their own research conform to the norms of modern science, (3) argue that their research is scientific but completely deform the definition of science, (4) consider science to be subservient to politics, or (5) argue that science is class-relative (Table 3). The philosophics, deductivists, and structuralists all take one or more of these positions. The materialists, on the other hand, accept the content of modern science and see their own research in these terms. They reject views about the relationship of class and science or politics and science which might jeopardize the quality of their research. This reinforces earlier conclusions to the effect that the materialists

**Table 3**
**Marxist Views of Science: Summary Statement for Chapter 4**

| Issue | Materialists | Structuralists | Philosophics | Deductivists |
|---|---|---|---|---|
| Modern science | Oppose *use*, not *content* of modern science<br><br>Science can be used to oppress, but it has a neutral core | Ambivalent<br>Criticize some aspects of modern science and praise others | Modern science is inherently oppressive<br>Science is contaminated by capitalism | Reject modern science because of its origins in the West |
| Do Marxists see their own research as being scientific? | Yes, same as contemporary social science | Yes, but redefine science as anti-empiricist and theoretical<br>Say their science is objective but deform meaning of terms "objective" and "science" | Three groups:<br>(1) No, opt out and don't do research<br>(2) Yes, their research could be scientific, but only after the revolution<br>(3) Yes, a science of the people or of the proletariat is possible—now! | Yes, see their own research as scientific but redefine science as dependent on dialectical and historical materialism |
| Relation of science and politics | Science is *not* subservient to politics | Natural science is *not* dominated by politics<br>Marxism replaces social science | Politics dominates science<br>Politics and science are fused<br>Political has priority over expertise | Officially, social science is subservient to politics, and natural science is not |

100

| Relation of science and class | Science is *not* class-relative<br>Reject the theory of two sciences | Reject the theory of two sciences<br>Science is *not* class-dependent<br>But the proletariat has a clearer view of some topics | There are two sciences: one is bourgeois and the other proletarian<br>Science is class-dependent | In reality, both natural and social science are subordinated to politics during certain historical periods<br>Marxism is said to be a science and able to substitute for other sciences including natural science |
| | | | Social science is said to be a class phenomenon; natural science is free of class influence | In reality the theory of two sciences is often applied to both natural and social science |

are more likely than the other Marxists to produce research of interest to non-Marxists.

Science, as presented in Chapter 1, is defined as central to the generally accepted model of research. Science is usually taken to mean the search for knowledge, the study of nature including human beings, represented by the accepted academic disciplines (Graham, 1981:3). Research is central to the scientific enterprise. It is one important way to discover knowledge, though no claim is made here that scientific activity itself can be used alone to justify the knowledge it produces, independent of purpose. Science assumes inquiry in line with the methodological and epistemological views discussed in the previous chapters. While it cannot provide clear, unambiguous answers to all questions, it is considered to be of potential use in improving the human condition. It is also understood to be independent of pre-given views that might in some way prejudice research results on an *a priori* basis. Therefore, contemporary social science rejects the premise that science is class-dependent or that politics can somehow impose either methods or results on the scientific enterprise.

## HOW MARXISTS VIEW MODERN SCIENCE AND HOW THIS INFLUENCES THEIR RESEARCH

Today it is difficult to produce defensible knowledge in the social sciences if the substantive content (body of knowledge) and procedural criteria (particularly those of verification and testing) of modern physical science are rejected. The scientific enterprise is commonly accepted to be one essential means for acquiring knowledge. Yet, as we will see in this section, all Marxists have objections to modern science as it exists in the West today. Does this militate against their being able to produce research of interest in terms of the assumptions of contemporary social science? This is indeed the case for most of the deductivists and philosophics and many of the structuralists who in one way or another either reject modern science or are critical of its central elements. But the materialists' objections are limited mostly to the way science is used rather than to its content or testing procedures. This keeps open the possibility that they can produce research acceptable within its terms.

The philosophics are so hostile to modern science that it would be almost impossible for them to do research acceptable in terms of its assumptions. They see it as inherently evil, a waste of time, of no value to society. They reject its conceptual framework and refuse to grant any special status to its knowledge claims. Their criticisms of science parallel their objections to positivism and empiricism. They maintain that science is uncritical, manipulative, mystifying, deceptive, authoritarian, alienating, dehumanizing, repressive, destructive, and a source of human misery. It is assumed to be an instrument of oppression that supports the status quo and serves to legitimize the interests of those who seek to dominate. The scars resulting from the bourgeoisie's domination of science under capitalism do more than just simply deform science; they produce a science with these objectionable characteristics.

Many of the philosophics confound science with technology, reason, and rationality, considering it an enemy to be defeated (Marcuse, 1969). According to this view, the content and method of science cannot be separated from its appropriation and its utilization (Horkheimer and Adorno, 1972). Science is never free of bias; it has no neutral core. Bob Young typifies this position in his article "Science *Is* Social Relations" (1977). Some of the philosophics call for the overthrow of science along with the capitalist system which they say supports it.

The philosophics' epistemological and methodological assumptions, examined in Chapters 2 and 3, are incompatible with those of science, and this too motivates them to reject it. They are idealist, voluntarist, anti-empiricist, anti-positivist, and subjectivist. Modern science is materialist, determinist, empiricist, positivist in many ways, and objectivist. Observable experience is central to the method of science; the philosophics deny the possibility of research based on this kind of evidence and substitute methods best described as interpretive and abstractly dialectical.

The deductivists also criticize modern science, most often using a selective combination of the same objections employed by the philosophics. But unlike the philosophics they do not condemn the idea of science itself because, as will be seen below, they hold aspirations regarding the scientific character of their own research. The deductivists' criticisms of modern science focus on its manifestations in non-Marxist, Western countries. One qualification is in order. During certain periods of crisis when production has been very important, the deductivists have temporarily suspended their denunciation of Western natural science. This does not involve the way they see social science and need not concern us at this point.

The Althusserian structuralists' view of modern science is not likely to promote their undertaking research according to the norms of the generally accepted model. These Marxists are ambivalent about modern science, favorable and critical of it at the same time. Althusser speaks in a highly positive fashion about science on the general level distinguishing it from ideology and emphasizing its objective character. But he is not referring to modern science as a whole and he does not recognize any general universal science. Neither does he have kind words for non-Marxist social science. Althusser faults modern science for its insistence on testing and evidence based on observation. He criticizes the supposed "infallibility that vulgar positivism ascribes to natural science," and rejects "even the probabilistic validity asserted by its more sophisticated exponents" (Blackburn and Jones, 1972: 44,150,153.). His praise is usually reserved for physics and mathematics and those branches of the natural sciences which they subsume (Althusser, 1971:42). This is not surprising since both have highly theoretical philosophical branches which depend on logic rather than testing. Althusser's apparently favorable view of science is more apparent than real. He reserves approval for a very special kind of science that confirms the priority he attributes to theory.

The materialist Marxists are predisposed toward a positive view of modern science because they share so many of its underlying epistemological assumptions: a reflective theory of knowledge, determinism, materialism, empiricism, certain elements of positivism, and a commitment to objectivity. The methodological assumptions of the materialists are equally compatible with those of modern science.

Because the materialists have a pragmatic, realistic view of modern science which allows them to produce research in line with its norms, they see science as conditional, incremental, tentative. They believe that it necessarily simplifies reality in order to study it. They argue that, although the agreed upon procedures and strategies employed by modern science do not guarantee truth, they have proved more helpful in producing useful knowledge than other kinds of non-scientific speculation or metaphysical means of gath-

ering information such as divine revelation, magic, witchcraft, folk-
lore, or mysticism. Scientific knowledge is more directly testable
in action than are the products of introspection, common sense, or
*verstehen*. Finally, for the materialist Marxists, science is not inherently oppressive but rather potentially liberating, a general human achievement (Bernal, 1939; Vaneau, 1979).

The materialists' do have objections to modern science, but their
criticisms do not constitute an absolute rejection of its approach
to inquiry. They distinguish between the substance, procedures,
and use of modern science, limiting their major criticism to the
way it is employed. They point out that science has often been
used by particular interests, by the dominant classes, as a means of
social control (Rose and Rose, 1976a:14), as a technique of paci-
fication and as a tool that is manipulated to preserve the status quo.
But they consider that although science can be distorted and deformed, it has a neutral core (Richta et al., 1968) that is valuable
for everyone (Osipov and Yovchuk, 1963).

In sum, any sweeping rejection of science and of its value to
society, any characterization of it as unequivocally oppressive, or
any identification of it as merely a tool in the arsenal of the enemy
reduces the likelihood of undertaking research acceptable within
the norms of the generally accepted model. The philosophics reject
modern science on these grounds as do the deductivists. The structuralists critique is more qualified. The materialists limit their criticism to the use rather than the method or content of modern
science, thereby allowing them to do research in terms of its norms.

## DO MARXISTS SEE THEIR OWN RESEARCH AS SCIENTIFIC AND, IF SO, IN WHAT SENSE?

Although all Marxists are critical of modern science, many of
them (all but a few of the philosophics) still seek to have their own
form of inquiry recognized as "scientific." But the validity of their
assertions about producing research of a scientific character is open
to question because, with the exception of the materialists, their
respective definitions of science differ from those required by the
norms of contemporary social science. Details of how the philosophics, deductivists, and structuralists redefine science so as to
give the impression that their own research is scientific are dis-

cussed below. Because the materialists' conception of science is more or less the same as that of modern science, outlined above, and because they see their research as conforming to its requirements (Szymanski, 1973:25), their views need not be described at any further length here but will be taken up again below in the discussion of the relation of science to politics and class.

### The Philosophics: Opting Out or Creating a New Science

The philosophics' hostility to modern science leads to a variety of responses with respect to how they define their own research, none of which promotes their undertaking inquiry that is valid in terms of the generally accepted model. One group of philosophics, of which Lukacs is an example, simply asserts the superiority of philosophy over science and retreats to the realm of reflection. Another argues that a science-of-the-people or of the proletariat, of a different character than that of modern science, is theoretically possible but that it can come into existence only in a post-revolutionary context where new forms of social relations have taken root. Marcuse takes this view. The philosophics who take these two positions seldom do research at all.

A third group of philosophics actually does undertake research but in a form that is compatible with their own epistemological and methodological assumptions and hence quite removed from the norms of contemporary social science. They argue that their research activity is scientific in the sense that it constitutes a kind of "new science" which is more or less the same thing as science-of-the-people, or what has historically been labelled in somewhat more popular jargon, a "proletarian science." These philosophics, however, call for its immediate implementation under capitalism. Many of the philosophics who actually do research in the science-of-the-people-tradition are academics (Bodemann, 1979; Young, Hovard, and Christie, 1977; Lacoste-Dujardin, 1977; Agger, 1977:48).

Habermas is an example of a philosophic who advocates "new science." He calls for an alternative science, an "emancipatory science," which is dialectical, critical, and democratic in character, which accepts subjectivity and relativism, which fuses the subject and the object, and which grounds science in "intersubjective communication" (Habermas, 1968). Habermas does not see much chance of this kind of new science being implemented within the context of present-day technological rationality, which he argues effectively curtails dramatic societal transformations.

All the philosophics who discuss science in connection with their research depart substantially from the definition of the generally accepted conception of science. Their understanding of new science is unlikely to lead them to produce research acceptable to most contemporary social scientists.

### The Structuralists Transform the Meaning of Science

The structuralists claim that their own research is scientific and objective. Indeed, they frequently criticize the philosophic Marxists as "relativist and unscientific" (Althusser, 1977:3–4). The structuralists claim that their science is a "rigorous, objective, theoretical form of inquiry." They say that it consists of an original system of concepts that are both definitional and objective, that are neither relative nor subjective. They argue that their research is scientific in the sense that it is opposed to speculation or sentimentalism. Structuralists see it as open-ended, the opposite of ideology which prejudges and is dogmatic and closed. They note that, whereas all science has its origins in ideology, Marx showed the way to break with this view and create an objective science apart from ideology (Althusser and Balibar, 1968:314) and they follow his example and direction.

In order to make the case that their own research is scientific the structuralists must transform the meaning of science in such a way that for all practical purposes they are doing something entirely different. Because the structuralists distort the term science and substitute their own version of it for that recognized by the generally accepted view, any research they produce within this new definition is not compatible with the assumptions of contemporary social science.

A closer examination of the structuralists' definition of science shows precisely how they deform its meaning. Their definition follows closely from their views of empiricism, observation, and theory outlined in Chapters 2 and 3. The resulting "science" is exclusively theoretical and intellectual, with no reference to concrete reality.

It is completely detached from sense appearances and does not seek to produce findings which can be compared with observable experience.

First, the structuralists say that because their science is structuralist in character it must be anti-empiricist and anti-humanist. For Althusser this means science cannot involve individual human beings employing research techniques, studying, experimenting, or observing reality, drawing conclusions, and formulating theories. What he calls "the subject role" (any function reserved for the individual practitioner in the research process) is absent from their inquiry.

Second, structuralist science searches for a structuralist reality that is "more true and authentic than appearances." Althusser states that this science designates a concrete reality, which, however, cannot be seen or touched (Althusser, 1971:75). The object of such scientific knowledge and the real object are two entirely different things (Althusser and Balibar, 1968:312).

Third, the structuralists' science is above evidence and need not be tested. It has no object outside its own activity. It is turned in upon itself and its own practice. Its only point of reference is its own norms and its own internal criteria (Lecourt, 1975:26).

The structuralists' understanding of modern science and their redefinition of it reflect a certain contradiction in their own thinking about inquiry which at once encourages them to undertake research in terms of the norms of contemporary social science and at the same time makes it impossible for them to actually carry out such research. On the one hand, at least formally, they see science as materialist in the sense that it makes a claim for objectivity, and is opposed to ideology; these characteristics encourage them toward concrete inquiry. On the other hand, their view of science is idealist in that it is anti-empirical and anti-experimental, exists independently of concrete reality, and is exclusively intellectual, taking shape only in the form of theoretical practice; this discourages their undertaking any form of empirically constrained research. In the next chapter we will see how this dilemma has led to a division within the ranks of the structuralists about how to do research.

## The Deductivists Transform the Meaning of Science

As with the structuralists, the deductivists say that their own research is truly scientific. And in order to make their case they, too, seek to redefine science in line with their own particular epistemological and methodological assumptions. The result is hardly more satisfactory than the efforts of the structuralists because once again the restructured science is unacceptable in terms of the norms of contemporary social science. The deductivists define science as any form of inquiry guided by dialectical and historical materialism. Thus, Stalin, for example, characterized any policy position taken by the Party as automatically the result of a "scientific examination of existing reality." The deductivists' science is not realistic, not tentative, not a corrigible effort based on increasingly adequate and improving information. It is, they say, accurate, veridical, and final because it is guided by the writings of Marx, Engels, and Lenin. Such an appeal to authority strikes at the very heart of the open-mindedness and willingness to bow to real world constraints that is central to the norms of science.

## MARXISTS ON SCIENCE AND POLITICS

Whether or not Marxists do research acceptable in terms of the generally accepted model is also contingent on how they understand the link between science and politics. All Marxists see science and politics as related in the sense that they reject neutrality and require political commitment or taking sides. But as was explained in Chapter 2, this does not necessarily preclude their being objective or their undertaking defensible research. Certain views about politics and science are, however, incompatible with the generally accepted model: the idea that science is subservient to politics, that the two should be fused, that a political view such as Marxism itself can ever substitute for science, or that political priorities should have more importance than technical matters in deciding how to actually carry out research. Those Marxists who take any of these positions risk compromising the quality of their research.

All these objectionable views of the relation between science and politics carry the risk that evidence may not be given a fair consideration or that the outcome of research may be limited in advance (before evidence is examined). This either deforms inquiry and transforms it into a deductive or dogmatic activity where research results are forced into the preconceived mold, or it restructures the research activity into an entirely different mode, that is, a political exercise.

### The Philosophics and the Deductivists: Politics Before Science

The philosophics and the deductivists give priority to politics over science, which further inhibits their producing defensible research. This section describes how those philosophics who do undertake research tend to fuse politics and science, or even to argue that politics dominates science. This leads them to put political commitment above technical expertise in carrying out research: the militant with high political consciousness is as important to the scientific enterprise as the person with technical proficiency. Consequently, the quality of the philosophics' research is called into question because putting politics above science eliminates the role of evidence in testing and transforms research into a form of political activity.

Two of the deductivists' views concerning the relation of science and politics pose particular problems for research. First, they maintain that science is subservient to politics. Their views on this matter are doubly complicated because they have a different perspective on this question for natural science and social science and also because, at times, their actual practice has differed substantially from the position they officially articulate. Second, they claim that Marxism itself can replace science. Neither position can be defended in the context of modern social science research.

With respect to the social sciences, the deductivists have given priority to politics with the consequence that social science inquiry has been required to accommodate its findings to the Party's political line. The Soviet deductivists put it most bluntly: "the fact is that sociology cannot stand outside politics, outside classes and the principle of partisanship" (Kozlovskii and Sychev, 1970–71:481). This view has made it very difficult for them to produce defensible research in these disciplines.

It is also useful to look at how the deductivists have treated the relations of politics and natural science because it offers a clear example of how making science subservient to politics can set back progress and remove research from the domain of what is commonly considered to constitute science.

Officially, the deductivists have maintained that social science is subject to political influence, whereas natural science, because it involves "man's collective mastery over nature," is not of the same political character. They state that natural science is unconsciously dialectical and materialist even when undertaken by non-Marxists.

The deductivists' stated principles concerning natural science and politics have *not*, however, been maintained consistently. At certain points in history, particularly during periods of calm when no international or domestic crises have been on the horizon and when any resultant decline in production could be tolerated, they have acted as if all science, both natural and social, should be subordinate to politics. For example, after World War II Lysenko's theories were given official party approval, though they were not solidly grounded in evidence, because they were said to follow logically from dialectical materialism. Those who disagreed with him were persecuted, tried, imprisoned, and in some cases even put to death. All science was similarly viewed as subservient to politics during the Cultural Revolution in China when political militants exercised a form of dictatorship over scientists. The deductivists in China argued that anyone could carry out research in the natural sciences without specialized training and that whether a scientist held "correct" political views was more important than his or her technical competence. In fact, professional proficiency was sometimes assumed to interfere with one's political development.

The consequences for the deductivists of considering either natural or social science to be subservient to politics are serious; it means that science must be reconstructed to conform to pre-given political views. Research results are deduced from political principles within this line of thinking. When politics dominates science, research is limited to demonstration or is transformed into an exercise of deduction and proof by logic. The result is dogmatism. If, as the deductivists hold, science is assumed to be valid only if it conforms with a particular political line, then there is no use in attempting to do research in terms of the assumptions of contemporary social science or to construct the empirical instruments needed for policymaking.

Another aspect of the deductivists' view of science and politics which has had disastrous results for the acceptability of their research is their attempt to substitute Marxism for science itself. For the deductivists Marxism is final, monolithic, "the greatest and the most important of all the sciences" (Cornforth, 1955a:143–44). It is an immutable truth, the only means to objective knowledge. Marx's dialectical materialism is presented as "a complete generalization of all science of nature and society" (Spirkin, 1975:32; Morgan, 1966). Marx is said to have discovered, as would any scientist, the laws of capitalist development and to have "scientifically substantiated them" (Aniken, 1975:382). Marxism, then, is assumed to have been proven, tested, and tried in practice just like any other science; it can be used to predict the future (Cornforth, 1969:147). For the deductivists, Marxism is an integral scientific system that contains an objective view of the world and a basic, non-empirical, scientific methodology grounded in dialectical materialism, universally valid for all substantive topics (Spirkin, 1975:32). This is called the "replacement thesis"; Marxism comes to substitute for science (Elzinga, 1977–78:2:2).

Because the deductivists attempt to substitute Marxism for science, it is almost impossible for them to produce research that is valid in terms of the generally accepted model. If Marxism replaces science, research is unnecessary. Anything of importance can be deduced directly from the approved doctrine. There is no need to look further for knowledge. In addition, if Marxism replaces science, then evidence that contradicts Marx's theories or the Party's policy must be ignored or suppressed and theory cannot be adequately tested, applied, and subsequently corrected. In such a context, any attempt at objective, independent study of reality becomes a dangerous proposal, for to undertake systematic research outside the pre-given opinion is to deny the legitimacy of the Party. If Marxism is permitted to substitute for science, the audience that will be interested in the results of any research undertaken within this set of assumptions is necessarily limited.

### The Structuralists: An Independent Natural Science and Marxism as Social Science

The structuralists' view of the relationship of science to politics is partly in accord with the requirements of the generally accepted model, and partly in contradiction with it. Consistent with their formal understanding of science as objective and the opposite of ideology, the structuralists argue that science and politics are separate. Althusser does not propose they should be fused. He retains a view of natural science as independent of Marxism. All this appears to be in line with the generally accepted model, even though, as shown above, the way the structuralists define the terms science and objectivity is questionable.

Althusser does however attempt to replace non-Marxist social science with Marxism. He first argues that there is not one science but several; math and physics are sciences. Second, he contends that Marxism is also a science. Like math and physics it has its own object and procedures (Althusser and Balibar, 1968:153). It has "the theoretical practice of a science" (Althusser and Balibar, 1968:32). Althusser does not formally argue all science is subservient to politics. He need not do so because for him the political view of Marxism is, by definition, an "objective" science. This position militates against the structuralists producing defensible research at least in the social sciences.

### The Materialists Refuse to Make Science Subservient to Politics

The materialists reject the idea that science is subservient to politics, thus conforming with the requirements of contemporary social science. They do not view Marxism as a substitute for science, and they believe that Marxism should be scientific in the sense of basing conclusions on evidence. Some materialists argue that socialism is the "administration of things." Therefore, they deny that science should be subservient to politics, or that political principles should have precedence over technical expertise in the field of science. Most of them give the edge to science over politics where such a choice is imposed. This does not mean that they think science has no political relevance. To the contrary, they argue for the necessity of political action based on the outcome of research, on a foundation of scientific knowledge (Barton 1971:462; Griffiths, Irvine, and Miles, 1979:368). Exceptions exist, however. Karl Kautsky and Rudolf Hilferding, both of whom were important precursors to the materialist current, actually proclaimed Marxism to be a science. But, for the most part, today the materialists' views concerning science are surprisingly consistent with the norms of the generally accepted model.

## MARXISTS ON CLASS AND SCIENCE

Contemporary social science rejects the view that science is class-determined and that there are two sciences, one for the bourgeoisie and one for the proletariat, because these views lead to a class-relativist position with respect to science. This means, ultimately, defending the value of knowledge resulting from science on the basis of the class origins of its exponents or the class character of its findings. If science is class-relative, at best it functions on the basis of preferences and, at worst according to simple prejudice. Such a science cannot provide the empirical instruments required for policymaking, those that inform us of the predictable consequences of action.

The Marxists' understanding of the relation of class and science parallels their view of science and politics. The philosophics and the deductivists assume perspectives opposed to those of the generally accepted model. The materialists support views that are more in line with it. The structuralists fall somewhere in between the two extremes. Many philosophics and deductivists regard science as class-relative or class-dependent and advocate the theory of two sciences in one form or another. The materialists reject this view; the structuralists are ambivalent.

### The Philosophics and Deductivists: Science Is Class-Relative

Both the philosophics and the deductivists adopt a class-relativist view of science, though each does so in a different way. As a result, each takes positions that are in substantial disagreement with those of contemporary social science. Because of their understanding of the relation of class and science, the research they produce cannot be considered acceptable in terms of the norms of the generally accepted model.

Most philosophics believe science is class determined in one way or another (Piccone, 1971:17). Those who do research and argue for a science-of-the-people or a proletarian science often describe science in class-relative terms requiring that it be guided by an expression of proletarian consciousness, that is, defined as an awareness of one's oppression in terms of economic deprivation, racial or gender discrimination, and so on. Certainly, these are not all classic Marxist formulations of proletarian consciousness. But many of the philosophics are neo-Marxists in the sense that they define the proletariat broadly. They claim that their new science is true because it is based on personal experience gained by the people or the proletariat in daily life experience or in class struggle. The logic of their argument leads to the acceptance of the theory of two sciences wherein there is a "true" science of the people and a false, misleading science of the bourgeoisie.

There is substantial weakness in the argument advanced by those philosophics who see science as part of the class struggle and who judge its truth value in an *a priori* manner, linked to a class view. Making science dependent on a class position is relativist and unacceptable in terms of contemporary social science. The line of reasoning underlying this view was outlined in chapter 2 in connection with the discussion of objectivity and class perspective. To summarize it briefly, only proletarian science is said to be capable of a dialectical view, of presenting a universal perspective on reality, because only the proletariat (defined broadly) has no interest in presenting a distorted image of the social, political, and economic conditions in society. The working class or the proletariat is assumed to have an epistemologically privileged position, a clearer, more accurate, less mystified, and less ideological view of society (Lowy, 1973:200–36). Only proletarian science truly reflects the objective movement of history and helps advance or retard it. Therefore proletarian science or the related science-of-the-people is superior to bourgeois science.

The deductivists also view science as class-relative; consequently, their research suffers. As with their understanding of politics and science, they argue that in principle the social sciences are class-dependent but the natural sciences are above class. Once again, at certain points in history they have acted as though all science, natural and social, was class-determined. The deductivists have never permitted the social sciences to escape the burden of being class-relative. They accept the theory of two sciences, and, historically, in the socialist countries, they have openly aided what they believed to be proletariat science, or as they now label it, "socialist sociology" (Kozlovskii and Sychev, 1970–71:478), and have suppressed anything considered to be bourgeois science. This view is expressed clearly in the pages of the French Communist Party's periodical entitled *Nouvelle Critique* (between the years 1948 and 1953). The French C. P. held a conference in 1950 devoted to the theory of bourgeois science and proletarian science and subsequently published a series of articles praising Lysenko.

At certain points the deductivists' views of class and science fuse with their understanding of science and politics, reinforcing the direction their inquiry must take. The logic of this convergence goes something like this. First, the Communist Party is defined as the principal representative of the proletariat and the main defender of its interests. Second, science is assumed to be class-relative and only proletarian science is considered to be true. Therefore, science must conform to the Party's political line.

The consequences of assuming science to be class-relative are clearer in the case of the deductivists than with the philosophics because the deductivists actually held political power and put their views into practice. Here the impact of the theory of two sciences was encountered in its most absolute form. The disastrous consequences of its implementation, not just for research but for production and for human welfare, are part of the historical record in both China and the USSR.

### The Structuralists and Materialists Reject a Class-Relative View of Science

The positions of the structuralists and materialists on the relation of class and science are close to those of contemporary social science. Both reject the view that science is inevitably class-dependent or class-relative or that there are two different sciences. On these points their assumptions about science parallel those of the generally accepted model and facilitate their doing research according to its norms.

Althusser and the structuralists deny any legitimacy to a class-based science but grant that the proletariat has a clearer view of some topics. They reject the theory of two sciences as it is generally formulated within Marxism. For Althusser, science is not an expression of proletarian consciousness or a summary of knowledge gained, by the proletariat, from the class struggle (Althusser and Balibar, 1968:141), but rather an objective theoretical structure. But Althusser does imply that the social sciences are pertinent to the bourgeoisie and what he calls the Marxist science of history, relevant to the proletariat (1971:7). He hints at a class-based science when he proposes that valid knowledge of class exploitation, repression, and domination in politics and economics will be recognized only by the proletariat. But he never directly defends a class-relative science.

The materialists today reject the view that science is class-dependent or that there are two different, class-based sciences, one proletarian and one bourgeois. Their only concession to this point is an admission that research produced within the terms of modern science is class-relevant (not class-relative) in the sense that it may be used by one class or another, that research results may be deformed or manipulated with a class goal in mind. The theory of two sciences is incompatible with their materialist theory of knowledge because the two-sciences theory implies that there are two, different class-dependent realities. This epistemological assumption leads them to argue that, although different views of the world are possible, ultimately there is only one science and only one real world to which science refers. They, therefore, contend that the bourgeoisie, even if it controls science in the West, cannot, in the long term, deform the basic knowledge of science itself. Science is not class-bound insofar as its purpose is to advance human knowledge about nature and society. The materialists argue that science is a "tool like any tool; it may be used in more than one way" (Cunningham, 1975:39).

The materialists argue that the economic and class relations in a nation may influence the development of science, but they maintain that the discoveries of science are not necessarily affected by class interests. Still, they hold that only under socialism, in a society where the interests of the proletariat are given preference, can the greatest promise of science as a positive, objective force for human advancement be realized, because only under these conditions would it be likely to be used to benefit the most people (Richta et al., 1968).

Historically, the materialists' rejection of a class-relativist science has not gone uncontested among their own ranks. Important precursors of modern materialist Marxism such as Bukharin argued for the theory of two sciences and for the class character of the social sciences (Bukharin, 1925:x-xi).

## CONCLUSION AND SUMMARY

Doing research involves assumptions about the meaning of science and its relation to politics and class which are so fundamental that rejecting them calls into question the very possibility of producing knowledge within the framework of contemporary social science. The philosophics and deductivists reject modern science and do not relate their research to that tradition. The structuralists are ambivalent about it, criticizing some of its principal assumptions, praising others. The materialists have a realistic understanding of modern science, accept its definition in terms almost identical to those of contemporary social science, agree with most of its assumptions, do not dismiss its potential value to society, and limit their criticism to the use of modern science rather than to its substance or procedures. They are comfortable with the idea that their research is part of this larger scientific enterprise.

Not all of those Marxists who reject modern science give up all aspirations for the scientific character of their own research. But in almost every case when they make the argument that their research is scientific they do not use the expression as it is generally understood but rather distort the definition of science so that it is meaningless. Given how they define science, it is very difficult for the deductivists, the structuralists, and the philosophics (for all the Marxists except the materialists) to undertake research in terms acceptable to contemporary social science.

Not all the philosophics agree on whether their own research can be considered scientific. There are three positions within philosophic Marxism on this question. One group asserts the superiority of philosophy over science and completely opts out of any attempt to do research of any kind. A second group contends that a science-of-the-people or a proletarian science is worthwhile, but they are pessimistic that such a science is possible before a dramatic revolutionary change in social relations, that is, in a post-revolutionary situation. A third group says that such politically engaged forms of "new science" as advocated by the second group are not only a goal, but can and should be implemented immediately. None of the philosophics argues that their research is scientific in the sense assumed by the generally accepted model.

Both the structuralists and deductivists make assertions about the scientific character of their respective research programs; however, both groups twist the meaning of science so that it differs substantially from that of contemporary social science. The structuralists reject any attempt to make their own research conform to the norms of modern science. Rather they redefine science (as anti-empiricist and exclusively theoretical), transforming its meaning such that it conforms to their own epistemological and methodological assumptions about inquiry and then claim that their research is "scientific" within the terms of this new definition. As the deductivists use the term, being scientific merely means being in agreement with what Marx, Engels, and Lenin wrote and in conformity with historical and dialectical materialism. Given their views on science, it is hardly likely that any of these Marxists would produce defensible research in line with contemporary social science or useful for policymaking.

How Marxists view the relation of class to science on the one hand and politics to science on the other is critical for research in the sense that certain positions on these subjects completely close off any possibility of producing defensible research. Those Marxists, such as the deductivists and philosophics, who say that science is class-relative (who accept the theory of two sciences), who fuse science and politics, who make science subservient to politics, who say that Marxism can substitute for science (as do some of the deductivists and the Althusserian structuralists with respect to social science), or who argue that political views are more important than technical expertise in undertaking research, automatically reject science as understood within the terms of contemporary social science.

In conclusion, the materialists' views of the relation of science to class and the relation of science to politics are more similar to those of the generally accepted model than any of the other Marxists. The structuralists' understanding of science, even though they deform the definition of science itself, includes a rejection of the class-relative character of science (the theory of two sciences) and, at least theoretically, a refusal to subordinate all science to politics. This brings them closer to the norms of the generally accepted model than the deductivists or the philosophics. As a result, the materialists are most likely to undertake defensible research; the structuralists are more likely to do so than the philosophics and the deductivists whose views of science compromise the possibility that they can produce research of use in defending knowledge claims and relevant for policymaking.

# 5.

# HOW MARXISTS DO RESEARCH

Chapter 5, first, explains how contemporary Marxists study social phenomena in terms of the research strategies and research techniques they employ. Second, it describes how their choices in these matters are influenced by their assumptions concerning epistemology, methodology, and science.

If research is defined broadly, as a fairly general kind of activity, as a synonym for inquiry, then most modern Marxists can be said to do research of one sort or another. But they do not agree as to what research involves or exactly how to go about it. The goal here is to determine which Marxist groups understand and carry out inquiry (1) recognized as defensible by contemporary social scientists and (2) likely to supply information for shaping the empirical instruments needed for policymaking.

To say that most Marxists do research in a broad sense is not to say very much. More important is the character of the assertions they make, the kind of evidence they produce, and how the knowledge that results from these studies can be used. The general model outlined in Chapter 1 refers to a set of assumptions used to determine the relative adequacy of the evidence and reasoning for the assertions made. It provides the link between the research activity and the claims made for the knowledge that results. In this chapter attention is focused on the research activity, the production of knowledge, rather than on the consequences, application, and usefulness of this knowledge. The latter are discussed in the next chapter.

As will be shown here, the philosophics, the structuralists who remain loyal to Althusser, and the deductivists all reject the research strategies of contemporary social science and propose alternative ways of doing research which are unlikely to satisfy the requirements of the generally accepted model. The philosophics politicize the whole research process. They use research as an excuse for political activity involving the creative potential inherent in this process in an effort to construct a new reality that did not exist previously. The kind of research the deductivists conduct amounts to little more than the dogmatic application of pre-given doctrine. They are unable to move beyond a view of inquiry as just another element in a complex of control mechanisms. The Althusserian structuralists understand research in strictly intellectual terms.

The materialist Marxists and those structuralists who reject Althusser's views use the same general research strategies and techniques as do many non-Marxist social scientists. They consider research to be a process of discovering an independently existing reality, as part of the larger search for knowledge.

## THE PHILOSOPHIC MARXISTS CHOOSE QUALITATIVE, SUBJECTIVE RESEARCH STRATEGIES

Many philosophics do not do research of any kind. Neither do they make positive reference to the findings of other Marxists who do. Historically, many of these Marxists such as Lukacs, Sartre, and Marcuse have found philosophy to be sufficient unto itself.

When the philosophics do research, they generally select subjective, qualitative research strategies (not all of them original to Marxism by any means) and the research techniques associated with them, which involve assumptions about inquiry compatible with their own views of epistemology, method, and science. They reject the research techniques common to mainstream social science. An example of one form of research used by the philosophics, namely, action research, is provided below. It illustrates how the philosophics inevitably depart from the norms of contemporary social science. Briefly, action research attributes a participatory role to those being studied, politicizes the whole process of inquiry, and allows it to take on a class-relativist perspective.

## The Philosophics Reject the Research Tools of Contemporary Social Science

The philosophic Marxists have reservations about the principal research techniques of contemporary social science, including all quantitative research tools and, in addition, those qualitative techniques that use statistics and mathematics. In almost every case, their doubts about these research tools signal a disagreement between the philosophics' assumptions about inquiry and those underlying the research techniques of modern social science. The philosophics' critique of these research techniques is given close attention here because, as will be seen below, they choose their own research tools, at least in part, in reaction against those of mainstream social science.

The philosophics reject quantitative research techniques because they believe these tools of inquiry dehumanize people, presume a view of humankind as passive, exaggerate the predictability of human behavior (Gramsci, 1971:428–29), and underestimate the possibility of human intervention and purposeful action to change a situation (Heiple and Pozzuto, 1975:10–13). The survey interview is often cited as an example of a quantitative research technique that is impersonal and alienating to the person being interviewed, assumes people's opinions remain the same or change only very slowly, and takes for granted that individuals act predictably.

The philosophics argue that social surveys, small group methods, and sociometry, among other research techniques, are reductionist because they assume that an understanding of the whole can be obtained by adding up the constituent parts. These research techniques, as well as quantitative content analysis and laboratory experiments, are criticized for neglecting the historical aspects of a topic which are important for an adequate understanding of the totality. When Theodor Adorno, who himself had emphasized quantitative research tools in his book *The Authoritarian Personality* (Adorno et al., 1950), changed his opinion about them in the late 1950s and denounced empirical inquiry as "stupid, blind, insensitive, and sterile," he stated it was because these tools could not contribute to an understanding of society in its *totality* (Lazarsfeld, 1972: 173–74).

The philosophics reject quantitative research techniques because they consider them to be positivist and empiricist. They object to the assimilation of natural and social science, implied by the transfer of methods from the natural sciences to the social sciences; causal modeling is an example. They argue further that human behavior cannot be quantified in the sense assumed by positivism and empiricism. They object to quantitative research and certain qualitative research techniques for (1) attributing numbers to what are basically human attributes of a qualitative nature, (2) scoring these characteristics on a numerical scale, and (3) employing discrete categories of analysis. According to the philosophics, the use of math and statistics in the study of human beings is objectionable not only because it is positivist and empiricist, but also because it is deterministic (Zeleny, 1980:99–102) and anti-dialectical (Karmen, 1972:30).

The philosophics also condemn the research tools of contemporary social science because these techniques assume objectivity as a goal. The philosophics argue that information obtained, for example, from interviews and questionnaires in the context of the social survey cannot be objective. They say that these research techniques tap only superficial and misinformed opinion, what Marxists call false consciousness. This is so, first, because those individuals included in a survey sample are interviewed in isolation, away from friends and in an artificial social context, and therefore they do not have a chance to grasp the real significance of any particular question. Second, the closed format of most survey questions makes it impossible for people to express what they really mean and feel because they cannot answer in their own words and in the context they perceive to be relevant to the question.

The philosophics criticize all the major quantitative research techniques commonly employed in social science for assuming a distinction between the object and subject of research. The philosophics argue that the two must be fused. They, therefore, reject social surveys which involve a research team that prepares the questionnaires and a sample of individuals who respond to the questions. The same is true for other research techniques which consider the person doing the research and those studied as completely separate from each other.

The philosophics are skeptical about the use of quantitative research techniques for gathering information about what is going on below the surface. They often cite public opinion polls and voting studies as examples of research techniques confined to measuring and reporting on appearances because they focus on the obvious, the superficial, and the trivial.

The explanatory forms implicitly assumed by many research techniques are equally unacceptable as far as the philosophics are concerned. Some of these research techniques deny the validity of teleological explanatory forms. They are incompatible with the philosophics' view of dialectical explanation where everything is overlapping and interconnected. Causal path analysis, for example, assumes a direct relationship between a cause and an analytically separate effect. Analysis-of-variance models attempt to separate main effects from interactions. Both of these data analysis techniques (1) define variables to avoid overlap in their respective models, (2) present variables as separate unities, and then (3) discuss the relationship between these elements as if they were isolated from each other except for the specifically defined interaction permitted by the model.

The philosophics maintain that all such quantitative research techniques are, by definition, inappropriate for studying dialectical phenomena because they can only describe and predict social relations that are in a state of rest and that are not undergoing major change (Karmen, 1972:27). They argue that the kind of dramatic change implied by the dialectic can never be measured or predicted.

Finally, the philosophics criticize the research techniques of modern social science because they see them as manipulative and generally harmful to humankind. For example, experimental research techniques are said to involve "intentional manipulation" as researchers seek to study change by modifying specific variables. The philosophics consider this form of "intervention" to be objectionable because it constitutes an "artificial, alienating gesture" (Bodemann, 1979), a restriction of human freedom.

In sum, the philosophics reject the principal research tools of contemporary social science, most of which involve quantitative research, and the use of mathematics and statistics, including the social surveys (structured interviews and closed question format), public opinion polls, sociometric methods, quantitative content analysis, laboratory experiments, naturally occurring experiments, and data analysis techniques such as causal modeling and analysis of variance. The philosophics' misgivings about science in general (as explained in Chapter 4) and the research techniques of contemporary social science in particular, especially quantitative techniques, have led some of them to reject the idea of doing research defined even in the most general terms. They argue for the superiority of philosophy and devote their energies to this type of theory. But many philosophics have come to adopt or develop a research strategy and to employ research techniques that they find less objectionable and more appropriate to their assumptions about inquiry. They seek to do research in a context unlike that of contemporary social science, a context of an entirely different character. As we will see, however, the results of their research are not acceptable in terms of contemporary social science.

### The Philosophics Adopt Certain Qualitative Research Strategies and Their Associated Research Techniques

This section is purely descriptive. It outlines some of the research strategies and associated research techniques employed by those philosophics who actually attempt to do research, and it presents a composite picture of the philosophics' approach to research. Little account is taken of the numerous points of contention among philosophics, some of which are far from trivial. In the next section these research tools will be evaluated against the philosophics' own assumptions about inquiry as well as those of contemporary social science.

*The philosophics choose research strategies that are qualitative and subjective, inspired by a variety of approaches, some of which are not Marxist at all.* They include the research strategies associated with hermeneutics, symbolic interactionism, ethnomethodology, Freudian psychology, phenomenological sociology, and existentialism. All of these orientations have underlying assumptions which the philosophics share. Many of them were developed by non-Marxist sociologists who were themselves disillusioned with the positivism and empiricism implicit in the generally accepted model of research: its reputed lack of a humanist focus, its acceptance of quantification and computer technology and what they saw as the trivial character of the results it has produced. The philosophics do not merely adopt these subjective, qualitative research strategies. They seek to adapt them to a Marxist point of view (Freund and Abrams, 1976), using them to study, among other things, metaphysical and aesthetic questions, cultural concerns, political and personal struggles, psychology, and personality. Three of these research strategies, each of which has had a substantial impact on how the philosophics do research, will be briefly described.

Hermeneutics is especially interesting to the philosophics because it is "concerned with interpreting and understanding the products of the human mind which characterize the social and cultural world." Based, for example, on personal insight and exegesis of language and documents, it elevates these forms of communication to a position of central importance in the understanding of human society. Language turns out to be more than just a "system of symbols for labelling the external world; it becomes an expression of the human mode of 'being in the world' " (H.G. Gadamer summarized by Burrell and Morgan, 1979:237–38).

The research techniques of social or symbolic interactionism focus attention on the relationship between those studied, between the self and the subjects studied, and between the self and fellow social scientists. It examines interaction sequences, searching for the process by which meaning is assigned and symbols are interpreted in a given situation. It emphasizes direct, firsthand knowledge of the object of study.

Ethnomethodology looks at everyday life experiences, at the particular character of what are considered to be routine occurrences that are generally taken for granted. Human behavior in social situations and institutional contexts is explained as rule-following activity. But each person interprets rules differently and according to context. The "fixing of meanings is something actively *done* by the participants in a particular social interaction" (Papineau, 1978:96). The ethnomethodologist argues for the superiority of intuition as a methodology.

The specific qualitative research techniques most frequently employed by the philosophics in the context of the broader research strategies outlined above include participant observation, field work, certain types of case studies, life history (oral biography), qualitative content analysis, unstructured (open-ended) questionnaires, and in-depth interviews (Pilsworth and Ruddock, 1975).

Although the philosophics reject quantitative research techniques and give priority to qualitative research techniques, not all qualitative techniques are considered to be equally acceptable to the philosophics. They reject those that affirm the methodological and epistemological claims made for research in terms of the generally accepted model —such as objectivity, and the grounding of research by reference to empirical reality. For example, the philosophics are opposed to rigorously structured participant observation, to systematic field work, and to certain forms of descriptive case studies, life history, and content analysis if they employ quantitative or mathematical data analysis. The philosophics warn that qualitative research techniques must be monitored against possible misuse by other Marxist groups or non-Marxists who, for example, might compromise its character by introducing quantitative material into it (Bodemann, 1979:156–60).

### Assumptions About Inquiry and Their Impact on the Research Process

The philosophics' assumptions about inquiry examined in Chapters 2 through 4 influence how they actually do research. The philosophics adopt qualitative, subjective research strategies and their associated research techniques, in part because of their objections to the research techniques of contemporary social science but also because this approach is logically consistent with their own assumptions about epistemology, methodology, and science. The research strategies and the research techniques employed by the philosophics are in agreement with their basically idealist, voluntarist, subjectivist epistemology. They are compatible with their emphasis on the intellectual and theoretical aspects of their mainly dialectical and interpretative methodology which aims to provide truth directly from the senses, without the intermediary processes of empirically constrained observation, concepts, data, theory, and so on. These research tools imply a rejection of modern science as it is usually understood. They can accommodate the logical implications for inquiry of the philosophics' view of science as subservient to politics and class-related. *As a result of these assumptions and choices, when they do research, many of the philosophics (1) encourage the researcher to become immersed in the milieu being studied, (2) allow those being studied to participate in carrying out the research when these individuals are members of the proletariat broadly defined, and (3) leave room for the political aims of the research and its class perspective to become more important than the link between research and the production of knowledge.* Because of the assumptions which the philosophics make about research and the way they actually go about it, the "knowledge" that results is difficult to defend in terms of the generally accepted model and of little use in policymaking.

### Epistemological Assumptions of the Philosophics' Research Tools

The epistemological premises underlying the philosophics' research strategies and their associated techniques conform closely to the philosophics' own assumptions (see Chapter 2). They are grounded in idealism and voluntarism. They are people-oriented and humanist, rejecting determinism and any attempt to predict or explain human behavior in the sense of discovering the causes of social action. They focus attention on individual consciousness, on personal experience, on situational descriptions, on intentions, and on motivations. They see people as goal oriented, as seeking self-understanding, as capable of defining their own reality, as striving to create their social life, rules, and values without constraint. They emphasize the significance of free will, the importance of the active creative individual, and the ever present possibility of dramatic unpredictable change. They see knowledge about reality as possible only through personal, subjective experience. Qualitative research techniques contain implicit assumptions about the nature of people which coincide closely with the philosophics' own idealist theory of knowledge that assumes human beings are special and apart from nature.

The philosophics' research tools are compatible with humanism, voluntarism, and a view of humankind that permits reconstructing the organizational framework of research. In this process new roles are attributed to both the researcher and those being studied in an effort to eliminate the separation of the object and subject of research. The philosophics define those being studied as "the people," transforming them into active subjects rather than considering them objects in the research process. "The people" assume a new participatory role within the context of inquiry: helping to carry out the research project, collectively involved in deciding exactly how inquiry will be undertaken.

The relationship between the researcher and those studied becomes a "dialogue" between the two, and so research is said to be a learning process for all. The researcher ceases to impose his or her way of thinking on those studied and instead accepts their criticism and their suggestions for changes in the research program (Freire, 1972:162–63). The philosophics argue for a non-hierarchical and anti-elitist research organizational structure (T. R. Young, 1977:3). The basic traditional division of labor between manual and intellectual tasks within the research situation is modified. Those being studied are assumed to be capable of comprehending and overcoming their own domination, in part by taking control of all aspects of their life, including the research projects involving them.

The philosophics choose research tools free of the positivist emphasis on neutrality. None of their research techniques requires a detached observer who avoids any action or intervention that might modify or change the behavior of those being studied. The person carrying out a research project becomes actively immersed in the milieu being observed and gets involved in the everyday life of those being studied.

Qualitative research techniques may be used in such a way that they are non-reductionist and center attention on the totality, which is another important point for the philosophics. Case studies, field studies, and participant observation can be oriented toward this kind of global view. The research strategies employed also emphasize the possibility of discovering the totality through the individual inasmuch as the individual is said to "re-totalize" the universal in his or her "singularity" (Catani, 1978:8).

Qualitative research as defined and used by the philosophics is empirical in the sense that it focuses on concrete reality but this does not lead them to accept crude empiricism, general empiricism, or objectivity. These Marxists emphasize the subjective quality of knowledge resulting from their inquiry. For example, when ethnomethodologists examine how people perceive social action they make no claim as to the objective character of their findings (Leiter, 1980).

The philosophics attribute a subjective mood to the most elementary raw materials of research. For example, diaries and historical documents are understood as qualitative sources of information that provide material on the attitudes and aspirations of individuals taken in terms of their own personal definition of a situation (Smolicz, 1974). The research techniques of participant observation, field studies, and life history emphasize a personal representation of reality, a subjective construction of an individual's world, not an attempt at objective description.

### Methodological Assumptions of the Philosophics' Research Tools

The methodological assumptions implicit in these qualitative research techniques parallel those of the philosophics' interpretative and dialectical method discussed in Chapter 3. These research tools place little importance on induction which the philosophics find offensive because it is incompatible with their dialectic (Rossman, 1981:146). Qualitative research techniques understand observation to be an activity of creative construction by the human mind, a form of self-reflection and subjective interpretation, rather than an attempt to describe a situation external to the person doing the research. People are assumed to have a natural ability to somehow sense and feel the meaning inherent in their cultural manifestations and in their own language, in ways far better than can be achieved with the traditional research techniques of contemporary social science. Qualitative research techniques are said to permit subjective perception, to offer the "view from within" (Kohli, 1978:4–5). They focus on the personal meaning of social acts, and language used to communicate meaning, by describing the different realities that exist concurrently for various individuals. The interpretation of symbols becomes important for research. Qualitative research depends on insight, inspiration, introspection, intuition, empathy, *versteben*, personal inspiration or self-reflection, and the ability to understand personal meaning which inheres in a social context (Bruyn, 1966:89–102). It attempts to set down how people perceive behavior as social action, concentrating on individual motivation and intention. The knowledge that results from research differs from person to person and from place to place, so that it must be constantly reconstituted.

Qualitative research techniques emphasize that data are the result of an effort at human creation of a reality. The philosophics do not assume that data somehow reflect the real world in the sense implied by empiricism. People construct their own "data" and are said to reaffirm their humanity in the process. Interpretation involves the attribution of socially generated meaning to phenomena. The process is relative and subjective in the sense that each action has a different and unique point of reference.

Qualitative research techniques are open to those forms of explanation that are most important to the philosophics, namely, dialectics and teleology. They look beyond external causes and promote understanding of human behavior in terms of the actor's goals or intentions. Case studies, field studies, and participant observation are more adaptable to the philosophics' view of dialectical explanation because they can be focused on dialectical change and interaction at the macro level more easily and more directly than the quantitative research techniques common to modern social science (the social survey, sociometric methods, structured observation, and so forth).

### Views of Science Implicit in the Philosophics' Research Tools

The philosophics' qualitative research strategies and research techniques permit these Marxists to do research and to put into practice their views of science as subservient to politics, where science and politics are fused and science is class-relative. At the same time, when the philosophics use these research strategies, they do not aspire to provide information in terms that are acceptable to modern science.

The qualitative, subjective research techniques preferred by the philosophics make science subservient to politics and give preference to political priorities over technical expertise with respect to inquiry. The philosophics' views of science reinforce the epistemological implications of their research strategies outlined above because both lead to participatory research. The expert (the researcher) is *not* assumed to be more qualified in doing research than the politically informed members of the population being studied. Many of the philosophics contend that only if the masses participate in every aspect of the research and retain ultimate control to modify it at any point according to their interests, opinions, and needs, can the dualism between the expert and non-expert be overcome (Agger, 1977:54). If this does occur, then people can strive to do their own research and eventually eliminate the expert altogether.

Qualitative research techniques such as participant observation and field work are flexible and open-ended, thus permitting the philosophics who view science and politics as fused (political activity and research activity as indistinguishable) to do research so that the search for knowledge is not separated or isolated from political activity and attempts to change reality. Qualitative research strategies make it possible to gear inquiry not just toward gathering information, and advancing knowledge, but simultaneously toward political education, consciousness-raising, and the initiation of social, political, and economic change. Research in this sense constitutes what the philosophics call "praxis." It plays a dual role of inquiry and intervention, committed to the transformation of the status quo and an effort to directly and immediately produce a new, more desirable reality, to improve life conditions, and to satisfy human needs.

The research strategies adopted by the philosophics are compatible with a view of science as class-relative. Research becomes part of the class struggle. These research techniques include a participatory role for those being studied; at the same time, it is assumed that those being studied can be defined exclusively in terms of "the people" or "members of the proletariat," not the bourgeoisie. Because these research techniques make no claim to being objective, but rather emphasize subjectivity (except for those who argue that the proletariat point of view is, by definition, objective), they encourage the production of class-related research results.

### Summary

The philosophics' choice of subjective, qualitative research strategies and the research techniques associated with them reflect (1) a rejection of the research tools of contemporary social science and (2) a close correspondence between the philosophics' assumptions about inquiry with those underlying hermeneutics, symbolic interaction, and ethnomethodology, that is, idealist, humanist, voluntarist, subjective, and non-reductive. These research techniques imply views of humanity, of social reality in general, of data, of the process of interpretation, of explanatory forms, of research materials, and of object-subject relations that are different from those assumed by contemporary social science. They permit the philosophics to act on their views of science as subservient to politics and as class-relevant in the sense that research is removed from the control of experts alone, fused with political action, and its procedures and conclusions restructured along class lines, that is, made relevant to the proletariat. This has implications for the research context and requires innovations in the social relations of research (relationship between the researcher and those being studied). If research involves the study of creative human beings acting toward goals (teleology) in a world that is ever changing (dialectical) and is assumed to be open to construction on the basis of human will (voluntarism), then research must be participatory and the research organizational structure non-hierarchical.

### The Philosophics' Action Research or Participatory Research: An Example and an Evaluation

Action research or participatory research is an example of one kind of qualitative, subjective inquiry available to those philosophic Marxists who choose to actually do research. Although it conforms to their own assumptions about inquiry, the results of such a research project would not be considered acceptable in terms of the generally accepted model.

Action research or participatory research begins when the research team calls a public meeting in the geographical area where the study is to take place. A debate may be conducted, or several days of meetings with those to be studied may be arranged (Freire, 1972). Involvement may include participation in decisions concerning the project definition and its goals. Philosophic researchers do not go to these meetings with questionnaires already constructed in hand. They may, however, make specific suggestions as to research topics. These are discussed with the group that attends the meeting. Problems are explored, hypotheses are formulated, and necessary research instruments are developed collectively. Participation is direct, with immediate interaction and feedback. Modification of the research would be allowed at any point during the project (Lacoste-Dujardin, 1977).

In doing research, the philosophics try to understand things from the point of view of those studied rather than imposing their own perspective on the situation. If notes are taken at these meetings, someone from the group to be studied might assume the task. A representative of the group being studied is sometimes elected to work alongside the researcher throughout the project. The researcher may be personally involved in the many mundane tasks of data collection. Those studied would also aid in analyzing the data and in making decisions about the distribution of results. Conclusions are formulated, discussed, and modified at a public meeting (Bodemann, 1978).

Finally, an educational program based on the "dialogical" technique might be included as part of an overall strategy for change (Comstock, 1980:11). Its goal is to help the group come to a better understanding of the contradictions inherent in their life situation and to gain a clearer perspective on themselves. In some cases a project for future action is also outlined in concert with the population. Praxis, then, is an integral part of the research methodology (Colfax, 1970:82).

In the extreme, participatory research may be carried to the point where the researcher is completely replaced. Here research tools are modified so that ordinary people can undertake their own research without always having the researcher present. Research not only serves the political movement by adopting its point of view, but it is designed and carried out by those who are genuine supporters of the movement (Erlich, 1976:6).

There are so many variations on this type of research that it is clearly not the exclusive property of the philosophic Marxists. It has been used by Catholic missionaries in the Third World. The Red Guard experimented with it during the Cultural Revolution in China, integrating it into their general political education campaigns among the peasants and factory workers, even though it is clearly incompatible with the general deductivist character of that particular political period (Siu-Lun Wong, 1979:97).

The participatory role attributed to those studied, the politicization of the whole research process itself, and the emphasis on the class orientation of research make it very unlikely that the resulting knowledge will be recognized within the terms of contemporary social science and will be of value in policymaking. The philosophics' research is not without interest to those who share their underlying assumptions about inquiry, but for those who do not share their assumptions these subjective, qualitative research techniques and the results they produce would be considered trivial or virtually useless.

## THE DEDUCTIVISTS DO RESEARCH IN CONFORMITY WITH DIALECTICAL AND HISTORICAL MATERIALISM

The deductivists reject contemporary social science research strategies and techniques in principle, partly for political reasons (because of their origins and development in the West) but also because they disagree with the basic assumptions related to inquiry which underlie these research tools. Traditionally, the most important form of research undertaken by the deductivists has been textual exegesis of the writings of the founding fathers of Marxism or historical description guided by the writings of Marx and his successors. When the deductivists were in power during the Stalinist period in the USSR from the 1930s to the 1950s, research understood in terms of the generally accepted model was not tolerated (Weinberg, 1974:8). Neither was this kind of research permitted by the Stalinist-dominated Communist parties in Western countries. Only when the materialist Marxists were dominant (from the late 1950s through the late 1960s) was systematic social research along the lines of contemporary social science in the West encouraged. Since the deductivists have returned to positions of authority (in the early 1970s), they have once again discouraged this trend, contending that quantitative research was "in error" (Lysmankin, 1977; Roumiantsev and Ossipov, 1969). At the same time, they have made some effort to adapt specific Western research strategies to their own assumptions about inquiry (Cohen, 1982:45–46; Shalin, 1978; Mathews, 1978; Lane, 1970). The example considered here involves abstract systems analysis. The deductivists' attempts to restructure Western research techniques have not, however, often led to the production of defensible research results, likely to be accepted by others.

## Classic Forms of Deductivist Research

In the past, the deductivists viewed research as synonymous with the scholastic exercise of textual interpretation and not much else. As far as the deductivists were concerned, social science consisted mostly of historical analysis or it was subsumed under philosophy. It was limited to translating social phenomena and the process of social development into categories of dialectical and historical materialism and to explaining social transformation in light of the political principles of the Communist Party. The goal of inquiry had little to do with understanding reality. Rather, it involved the search for the correct formulation of theory in relation to historical and dialectical materialism or the "right" explanation of history with respect to what Marx or Lenin had said (Palmer, 1981:46–51). Such research was reserved for the specialists in the Academy of Sciences or in the Communist Party Central Committee. A certain infallibility was attributed to interpretations made by members of these organizations. The role of deduction in the process of research as textual demonstration consists of arguing on the basis of principles already accepted without reference to further evidence. The results seldom lead to new discoveries and are generally limited to self-confirmation of preestablished views. This kind of research activity achieved no broad recognition outside deductivist circles.

This view of research is not merely a relic from the past but is still actively advocated by many deductivists. In the 1970s as the deductivists regained influence in the USSR, their criteria for judging the value of research was that it be in conformity with the thought of Lenin, loyal to the fundamentals of Marxism, and "true" to the Communist Party. They have a conception of social research as requiring that one "apply Marxism in reality" (Kozlovskii and Sychev, 1970–71:478–81).

## The Deductivists React to Contemporary Social Science Research Techniques

The deductivists, geographically concentrated in the USSR and Eastern European countries, reject the research strategies of contemporary social science largely because they do not share the assumptions implicit in this kind of inquiry. For example, the deductivists claim that the research strategies of modern social science neglect the totality and give too much emphasis to the parts. Marx, they argue, required that society be examined as a "social organism, not as a sum of individuals.... The essence of the human being is the totality of social relations" (Kozlovskii and Sychev, 1970–71:479). The deductivists are also suspicious of quantitative research undertaken within the West because it concentrates too much on data while neglecting the theoretical aspects of a question and because it is too mathematical and statistical (Graham, 1972:236; Lewontin and Levins, 1976:39). Some deductivists even object that mathematics is inappropriate for the study of human behavior because it is grounded in formal logic and because it is too closely linked to Western "analytical philosophy and positivism." Stalin provided the basis for this view (Graham, 1972), discouraging social science inquiry based on data collection and analysis (Osipova, 1971:178–79; Hahn, 1977:37).

The deductivists' hostility to contemporary social science research in general and to concrete research in particular has undergone a slight modification in recent years, at least in the USSR (Slider, 1985). They are in a sense caught between an increasing realization of the value of contemporary social science research for purposes of legitimation and especially for policymaking, and the incompatibility of their own assumptions about epistemology, method, and science with this type of research. Although this change indicates a softening of the deductivists' opposition to social science research, it does not constitute a dramatic reversal in their position as regards research.

First, the deductivists have begun to cite and publicly report evidence from quantitative research produced in Western countries, if the results of these inquiries lend legitimacy to their own conclusions. Research results from Western sources which contradict their views continue to be either ignored or denounced as bourgeois.

Second, there is evidence that some of the deductivists themselves have undertaken research that appears to be recognized as acceptable in terms of the generally accepted model. But such research is required to be "totally subordinated to the interests of Party bodies and the need to improve the effectiveness of their work." It must assist "Party bodies in implementing the political line of the Party" (Alekseev, Doktorov, and Firsov, 1980:43). The topics that may be studied are closely controlled by the Communist Party (Slider, 1985:220). Published research deals with the family, education, leisure time, moral and ethical views, ethnic relations, and so forth. Certainly, research on these topics is not without interest to non-Marxists. But most often, only summaries of data are published, often in a form that makes it impossible to reinterpret data or to draw conclusions contrary to those offered by the original researchers. It appears that in the 1970s, after the deductivists consolidated power, only Party members, for the most part, were permitted to undertake concrete inquiry (Britvin, 1980–81:58). Those materialist Marxists who continued to do research during this period saw their autonomy severely limited and the ideological control of the content of research dramatically increased.

Research on sensitive topics such as the poor, the elite, the Party, political matters or ideology, the status of women, absenteeism, alcoholism, job dissatisfaction, the class character of education, reduced social mobility of the lower classes, alienation among urban industrial workers, any of which might yield findings that cast the government or Party in a bad light, was discouraged by the deductivists or, if permitted, the results were restricted to private circulation (Welsh, 1981). But throughout this period the Communist Party in the USSR has continued to make use of public opinion polls to measure the effectiveness of its own ideological work and to improve the content of its propaganda (Slider, 1985:213).

In some cases deductivist research amounts to organizing a research project in which the desired results are set out in advance and the data collected in order to illustrate the pre-given conclusions. When such "research" is reported in professional journals, details are seldom provided about the methods employed and the results are discussed only in the most general of terms. The consensus of Western scholars is that the deductivists deform inquiry as it is understood in terms of the generally accepted model. The deductivists' research activity in this case constitutes little more than a type of self-confirming activity.

A French Communist Party survey of its members is a good example of how the deductivists undertake research (Laurent, 1979). Apparently based on a total enumeration of its membership, the compilation of the members' background characteristics is presented without the methodological details of how the study was carried out. The cross-tabulations are presented in a misleading manner so as to "prove" that the Party is both "young" and "working class." The manipulation of the data is so evident that the article appears to be mere propaganda for public consumption rather than a serious piece of research.

Another way the deductivists have sought to resolve their ambivalence about social science research is by selecting some of the research techniques of contemporary social science and adapting them to their assumptions about inquiry. This "solution," illustrated by an example of how the deductivists have modified systems analysis, does not change the fact that they remain officially opposed to research as outlined in the generally accepted model. For them, historical materialism is still the general, overarching theory of social sciences.

### Abstract Systems Analysis as a Deductivist Research Tool

Today some deductivists encourage the use of their own adaptation of systems analysis and, to a certain extent, structural-functionalism as acceptable substitutes for the more empirically constrained inquiry of contemporary social science. In the early 1950s they attacked systems analysis because it was a product of the West; this alone was enough to make it unacceptable. Beginning in the late 1960s, however, the deductivists in the USSR began to formulate their own version of systems analysis, appropriate to their assumptions about epistemology, methodology, and science (Gouldner, 1970:Chapter 12).

In an attempt to establish the legitimacy of systems analysis in a socialist context, the deductivists argue that it has been part of Russian science since the beginning of the twentieth century (Blauberg, 1977:94). In addition, they contend that Marx "was the first to formulate the scientific conception of the systems nature of social phenomena" contributing much to its elaboration and development (Kuzmin, 1979:46; Blauberg, Sadovsky, and Yudin, 1977). They suggest that the logic and method of his greatest work, *Capital*, was very similar to that of systems analysis (Blauberg, 1977).

As a research strategy, Western systems theory is remarkably flexible, making it possible for the deductivists to redefine it as consistent with their assumptions about inquiry, their understanding of historical materialism, and their abstract view of the dialectic. The deductivists present systems analysis as an alternative to causal explanatory forms. "Systems methodology is one of the applications of the general methodological concepts of dialectics to specific material" (Blauberg, Sadovsky, and Yudin, 1977:9; Iadov, 1975; Ukraintsev, 1978).

The deductivists modify systems analysis to make it compatible with their idealist concept of the totality as "non-additive, irreducible and non-disjunctive" (Pushkin, 1980:272; Wiatr, 1979:13; Sztompka, 1979a:135–43). They understand it to be anti-elementalist and to focus on the macro-theoretical level (Blauberg, 1977:97–98). They interpret this to mean that it is consistent with an understanding of the Hegelian totality as an integrated, developing "social organism." It is said to emphasize the inseparable relations between the parts and the whole, the interconnection of the parts, and the priority of the whole in the last instance. It does not require that phenomena be simplified in order to be studied, as do so many other contemporary social science research strategies (Blauberg, Sadovsky, and Yudin, 1977).

As restructured by the deductivists, systems analysis is highly abstract. It emphasizes the theoretical and orients research away from what the deductivists consider the most dangerous aspect of contemporary social science, that is, concrete reality and observable experience. Their form of systems analysis assumes that data are unimportant and secondary to theory (Iadov, 1975), which conforms to the deductivists' view that social science concentrates too much on data and facts anyway (Siu-Lun Wong, 1979:69). Systems analysis becomes merely a complement to the deductivists' basic research strategy of demonstration on the basis of principles already accepted and considered to be self-confirming without reference to evidence. It cannot be used to examine such important matters as conflicts within society, contradictions between Communist Party policy and reality, or the need for change. This is safer from the deductivist point of view, as it does not require examining what is actually going on in terms of policy successes and failures and it does not threaten the bureaucracy (Hahn, 1977:54).

Systems analysis appears to be above politics, but because the deductivists have historically insisted that social science be subservient to politics, they employ it so that it submits to their political goals. Systems analysis does not call into question the hierarchical decision-making structure that characterizes so many Soviet institutions. It is applauded by the deductivists because it is said to encourage the movement of information "up the chain of command without relinquishing the dominant role of central authorities and the Communist Party in the policymaking process" (Kelley, 1977:1212; Schwartz, 1973:247).

Systems analysis is compatible with the deductivists' assessment of the political needs of developed socialist states at this point in time, emphasizing consolidation rather than revolutionary transformation (Kalab, 1969b). It is concerned not with conflict and change, but rather with the stability of a system. It focuses on what actually exists and thus legitimates the status quo. Conflict is understood to be dysfunctional. The deductivists seek in it a scientific basis for containing conflicts and achieving an equilibrium. The functional and integrative aspects of the system are a central focus. The mechanism that guarantees the preservation of the qualitative specificity of systems is set forth, as well as their function and development (Afanasyev, 1979:27–38).

Systems analysis is not without its critics among the deductivists within the USSR. Some deductivists claim that it may deform the Stalinist tradition (Lektorsky and Melyukhin, 1977; Schwartz, 1973). Others have insisted on integrating a class component into it. Still others mention the necessity of orienting systems analysis toward history. The struggle to distinguish it from its use in the West continues (Blauberg, 1977:928).

At this point in time, it is impossible to predict if systems analysis will be rejected or accepted by the deductivists in the long run and, if it is accepted, the exact form in which it will be incorporated into deductivist Marxism's repertoire of research techniques. Inasmuch as the deductivists now employ systems analysis as an abstract model independent of all empirical constraint, it is not of use in producing theory that can serve as a basis for prediction. Its conclusions are not tested against reality or empirically constrained in any way.

## THE STRUCTURALISTS EITHER ABANDON ALTHUSSER OR
## DO RESEARCH AS AN EXCLUSIVELY INTELLECTUAL ACTIVITY

Despite the fact that structuralist Marxist assumptions about inquiry are incompatible with all forms of contemporary social science inquiry, many of them have produced some interesting and important research acceptable within the terms of the generally accepted model. How is this to be explained? This section shows that two groups exist within structuralist Marxism. Some structuralists remain faithful to Althusser's views, reject the research tools of contemporary social science, and the qualitative subjective research techniques of the philosophics. Instead, they seek to substitute research techniques that are more appropriate for their assumptions, though most often the results are useless from the point of view of contemporary social science. Other structuralists have chosen (1) to simply ignore Althusser's assumptions about inquiry that conflict with research in terms of the generally accepted model, (2) to emphasize those aspects of his views that appear to be compatible with this model, and (3) to carry out research recognized as legitimate within the norms of contemporary social science. Certain characteristics of Althusser's assumptions about inquiry make this possible, as does his inconsistency with respect to his own position in these matters.

### The Althusserian Structuralists Reject Both
### Contemporary Social Science Inquiry and the
### Philosophics' Qualitative Approach to Research

The structuralists who retain an Althusserian point of view oppose research in terms of contemporary social science. Their assumptions about inquiry make it equally impossible for them to take the line pursued by the philosophics and to adopt subjectivist, qualitative research strategies. When the structuralists do research, they search for macro-level structures or turn to abstract textual analysis. An example, discourse analysis, is given below.

The structuralists reject the empiricist research strategies of contemporary social science that focus on the individual (rather than on structures) and recognize the utility of historical variables. Althusser objects to the empirically constrained character of modern social science methodology and the resulting theory grounded in evidence because of his epistemological view outlined in Chapter 2 concerning the superficial character of what can be directly observed. In addition, modern social science research techniques focus on specific individuals in particular places performing concrete actions. There is no place in a structuralist analysis for the subject (individual human beings), the conscious will of individuals, their actions and their private undertakings (Althusser, 1965:228). Such an approach is denounced as humanist. Althusser criticizes the way the research techniques of the social sciences treat historical variables as well. He rejects any attempt to look at history in terms of events or individual actors, and he substitutes a structuralist view of history as "a process without subjects." (By this he means history without people playing specific roles.)

These Althusserian structuralists cannot, as did the philosophics, adopt more subjectivist, qualitative research techniques as a substitute for the research tools of contemporary social science. The philosophics' subjective, qualitative research techniques make assumptions incompatible with the structuralists' anti-humanism and their denial of the importance of the creative human subject. Given their views on these matters, few research strategies remain open to them.

The Althusserian structuralists make assumptions about epistemology, method, and science which encourage a shift away from the search for causes of social phenomena (which focus on events and individuals) and a move toward, on one hand, macro-level structures that are not directly or immediately visible and, on the other hand, a textual mode of analysis on an abstract level. Neither of these is accessible with the research tools of contemporary social science. The Althusserian structuralists, therefore, have little choice but to define research as abstract intellectual theorizing and to choose research techniques appropriate to this point of view. In certain forms discourse analysis and semiotics (the study of signs) are research strategies acceptable to them.

### Discourse Analysis: An Example of How the Althusserian Structuralists Do Research

Opportunities for undertaking research consistent with Althusser's assumptions about inquiry occur only rarely and are severely limited in terms of their potential; one such effort involves discourse analysis. It is a modified version of a substantially more abstract character of what is commonly known as content analysis. Its assumptions, however, are congruent with the Althusserian structuralists' premises about inquiry. It is used to examine symbols rather than events or ideas. It draws attention to the absurdities, the discontinuities, and the errors in a communication, to what is left unsaid, to what is hidden or omitted in a text rather than to what is made explicit. The slips and silences of the written word are assumed to express an unconscious reality (Callinicos, 1976:36). The works of Michel Foucault are an excellent example (1971; 1972; 1976). Seeking to go beyond the conscious level, discourse analysis assumes that what is absent from a communication is more significant than what is obvious in it because the missing elements provide clues to the hidden structural reality lying beneath the surface. Discourse analysis as understood and employed by Althusser's successors substitutes the study of language as a universal symbolic system for a broader study of social reality, taking on an anti-empirical, highly theoretical expression, concentrating on the form and the structure of what is communicated, but neglecting the agency and the content of a statement. When defined in this manner, it risks "treating social reality itself as a discursive order, rather than as a reality external to discourse but to which discourse refers" (Lovell, 1980:29).

The Althusserian structuralists agree with the underlying assumptions about inquiry implicit in discourse analysis. They are enthusiastic about its epistemological premises because, for example, it orients inquiry toward the whole without neglecting the parts. A communication is viewed in its social, political, and economic context, as "a process without a subject" (Pecheux, 1975:180), which means no attention is paid to specific individuals. It is compatible with the structuralists' methodological assumptions because, for example, it emphasizes abstraction, it views research as a process without any link to empirical observable reality, and it seeks to attribute meaning in a situation where the constraint of evidence is consciously ignored. It does not search for historical explanation (temporal antecedents) or causal explanations. It is consistent with the structuralist view of science as exclusively a form of intellectual reflection.

The Althusserian abstract form of discourse analysis makes assumptions about reality which are inconsistent with the generally accepted model. Research such as discourse analysis substitutes a text for reality, the invisible for the concrete, and at the same time eliminates subjects (human beings) as agents of change.

### Abandoning Althusser: The Who, Why, and How of Dissent

Some structuralist Marxists have abandoned Althusser and have begun doing research in terms of the norms of the generally accepted model and of use in constructing the instruments required for policymaking. Notable among them are Nicos Poulantzas, Maurice Godelier, Erik Olin Wright, Michel Verret, James O'Connor, and Manuel Castells. These and other structuralists who share their view have come to link their research to observable experience. They accept the fact that theories must be constrained by reference to statistics and data, tested against evidence, and corrected on the basis of new information. This has not been difficult for them to do because (1) Althusser's form of structuralism includes research-relevant assumptions that appear, at first glance, to be consistent with the generally accepted model and (2) Althusser has contradicted himself about how to do research and thus leaves the way open for those who question some of his views.

On at least a formal level, Althusser appears to accept certain elements of the generally accepted model: a mixed theory of knowledge; some elements of positivism; structural determinism; objectivity; structural causality; a view of science as objective (the opposite of ideology), not entirely subservient to politics, or completely class-relevant. In most cases Althusser's position on these topics only appears to be the same as that of contemporary social science; further inquiry reveals that his definitions of some of these terms diverge markedly from normal usage in social science. Many structuralists have simply elected to overlook this, to take his views on these topics as if they really were close to those of contemporary social science, and to neglect the aspects of his assumptions about inquiry which are openly hostile to contemporary social science.

On some occasions, Althusser has publicly and privately contradicted his own assumptions about research. This has encouraged some structuralists to question certain of his views and yet still remain structuralists. In his self-criticism (published in 1976), he revised some of the positions he had previously defended very strongly, most importantly, the emphasis on the theoretical. But even before this date, in the late 1960s, there is evidence of Althusser's confusion and inconsistency about the assumptions of inquiry. In his letters to Maria Macciocchi, a personal friend who was undertaking research in Italy, he stated positions contradicting his published opinions in response to her questions about how to go about inquiry. He encouraged her (1) to undertake an empirical form of fact gathering, to use statistics whenever possible, (2) to focus on what individuals say, letting "the people speak themselves," and (3) to emphasize an historical perspective in her field work (Macciocchi, 1969:21, 297–98). He told her that data, be they obvious, factual, and immediately visible, were not only suggestive but also essential for a comprehensive understanding of what was going on. These views are more than simply "plurality within discourse." They are inconsistent with Althusser's rejection of empiricism, and his doubts about the utility of observation. They contradict his understanding of reality in terms of structures rather than individual human beings. Althusser appears to have begun to doubt his own form of structuralist Marxism long before his successors started to question it. The publication of this correspondence may have encouraged some of the structuralists influenced by Althusser to reconsider their assumptions about inquiry.

On the one hand, few of the structuralists who abandoned Althusser bothered to formally draft a different set of assumptions about inquiry as an alternative to Althusser's view of structuralism within a Marxist framework. They have simply set about doing research, in line with the generally accepted model. They often retain the structuralist paradigm and language in introducing their research, and they frequently present their conclusions in terms of a structuralist theoretical framework. At the same time, *these structuralist Marxists implicitly concede something that is completely unacceptable to Althusser, namely, that observable experience offers clues to what is going on at the structural level.*

On the other hand, some of the structuralists who have abandoned Althusser and have undertaken research in terms of the generally accepted model are aware that it is necessary to modify some of his premises about structuralist Marxism. For example,

Poulantzas' view of the totality stresses the relative autonomy of the parts of the totality. The whole is less of an abstract concept for him, more of a concrete reality, resulting from the various structures and their interplay. Partial statements about the totality are treated as pertinent and important. Distinct empirical reference to the various parts of the whole becomes a meaningful way to constitute knowledge (Poulantzas, 1973; 1978).

The research produced by the structuralists who have abandoned Althusser is of significantly more interest to non-Marxists who agree with the generally accepted model than is the research produced by those structuralists who remain faithful to Althusser.

## THE MATERIALISTS DO DEFENSIBLE RESEARCH

The materialist Marxists go about research much as required by contemporary social science. The assumptions they make concerning epistemology, method, and science are congruent with the premises of the generally accepted model. The research they produce is, therefore, of considerable interest to a non-Marxist audience.

### The Materialists Adopt the Research Strategies and Techniques of Contemporary Social Science

The materialists use the research strategies and techniques of modern social science without hesitation, namely, statistical analysis, quantitative research techniques, and certain types of qualitative research tools. Many materialists even make use of such pillars of contemporary social science as the social survey, questionnaires, structured interviews, quantitative content analysis, rigorous field studies, concrete life history reports (Bertaux, 1976), in-depth interviews, certain types of case studies, sociometry (Mandic, 1967:454), systematic forms of participant observation, and a type of cybernetics that focuses on concrete evidence (Graham, 1964). As the materialists define these research techniques, they all refer to experience that is, directly or indirectly, observable. The materialists have no objection to the use of computers in research (Bodington, 1973) or to describing human behavior and attitudes in terms of mathematics or statistics. They understand quantitative research techniques provide summary statements which, when used appropriately, may facilitate comprehension of the complexity of the world around us. The materialists seldom use qualitative research approaches and techniques that are based on idealist epistemological assumptions (symbolic interactionism, ethnomethodology, existentialism, and so on).

The very existence of Marxists who do research in this manner may be surprising to many non-Marxists who are unfamiliar with the materialist current within the Marxist tradition. Historically, the philosophic Marxists who oppose research in terms of the generally accepted model have been dominant in the West. Over the last few decades there has been a renewed interest in the materialist Marxist orientation which requires attention to data and testing. The trend began in Europe earlier than in North America (Birnbaum, 1971); it is geographically more in evidence in the United States and Great Britain than in France or Southern Europe today (Anderson, 1984:20–23).

In the 1960s the rise of Euro-communism together with Moscow's more open attitude on the question of contemporary social science research encouraged official Communist parties outside the USSR, even in Europe, to devote resources to research. Party research was used to assess the political strength of candidates, to plan effective electoral campaigns, and, if elected (at the municipal level in Italy, for example), to provide information needed to govern effectively.

A materialist Marxist current has existed during certain historical periods in socialist countries as well, though the deductivists contested its very existence (Osipova, 1971; Szczepanski, 1966). In Eastern Europe and the USSR from the 1930s through the 1950s, either fascist influence or Stalinist leadership effectively destroyed most of the institutional structures that could have supported modern social science. This prohibited its rapid reestablishment after the materialists took control of research policy when Khruschev came on the scene. Although many East European countries were affected by the trends in the USSR, some showed independent patterns of development. In the case of Yugoslavia, the materialists returned to power soon after Tito denounced Stalin in 1948 (Spadijer, 1979:137), and this aided the development of social science in that country. Poland has also remained relatively more independent of trends in the USSR and so preserved a continuity of social research more effectively than was the case with the other Eastern Bloc countries. The return of social science research was slowest in East Germany, Bulgaria, and Rumania (Leon, 1971: 157–59; Denitch, 1971).

The materialist Marxists in socialist countries and especially in the USSR turned to Western social scientists to help reconstruct a social science research capacity in these countries in the 1960s. This certainly reflects the way they viewed inquiry. Talcott Parsons, Robert Merton, Lewis Feuer, and Raymond Aron were among the first Western sociologists invited to Moscow for consultation (Parsons, 1965). In a similar manner as materialists gained influence in post–Mao China in the late 1970s, Western scholars were brought in to help reorganize Chinese social science (Social Science Research Council, 1979; Institute of Social Research, 1981).

Some examples of the research topics studied by materialist Marxists in the West and in the socialist countries indicate the range of topics that preoccupy them and are of help to non-Marxists in locating Marxist research of interest. In the West they study capitalism, the state, the bureaucracy, the economy, the relationship of politics to economics, imperialism, class structure, class conflict, workers and trade unions, and so on.

Concrete historical studies in line with this orientation have shown so much dynamism and growth as to merit special mention. Perry Anderson summarizes work in this area (Anderson, 1984:21–27). Richard Edwards' history of the social relations of the work place and the development of managerial mechanisms of control is an additional example (Edwards, 1979). The author uses a variety of types of concrete evidence in relation to his hypotheses, including statistical summaries, census data, interviews with workers and management, and content analysis of internal company documents.

In the socialist countries, materialist Marxist research covers the transition from private forms of ownership to new types of public ownership, the effect of different types of incentives on production, how to increase factory efficiency in general, how to incorporate minority and ethnic groups into mainstream society, how to increase economic development, how to make administration and management more effective, how to improve relations between urban and rural sectors of the population, how to increase social mobility, and how to deal with social problems (crime, juvenile delinquency, population control, alcoholism, and so forth). They have studied topics such as job dissatisfaction, work alienation, economic inequality, and class bias in education (Lavigne, 1968; Zivkovic, 1969: 121–22; Shalin, 1978:180; Osipov and Yovchuk, 1963:222–23; Lysmankin, 1977:21; Kelley, 1977:vi; Hahn, 1977; Solomon, 1977:18, 30).

The materialists do not uniformly embrace all the research techniques of contemporary social science just as they are. Those materialist Marxists who use them do not always employ them in exactly the same way as non-Marxists. But, as will be seen below, the modifications they have brought to these techniques are relatively minor, relating to their Marxist theoretical preoccupations rather than to the character of the research techniques themselves.

### Research Techniques and the Materialists' Assumptions about Inquiry

The materialists' assumptions about epistemology, method, and science are consistent with the underlying premises of most quantitative research techniques and certain qualitative research techniques common to contemporary social science. Hence, they have little reason to avoid using them for their own research. Although they did not invent these research techniques and have contributed little to their development, the materialist Marxists argue that in the majority of cases there is no contradiction between their own Marxist views and the use of these research techniques.

From an epistemological point of view the materialists assume that reality exists apart from knowledge about it. The research tools they employ from the social survey to quantitative content analysis are designed to systematically investigate a world that exists independently of the act of inquiry itself.

Because their epistemological assumptions do not attribute special properties to human beings which require that people be studied differently from the rest of nature, the materialists are not uncomfortable, as were the philosophics, with the organizational structure of contemporary social science research. The materialists, therefore, do not emphasize the participation of those being studied in the research project. For reasons of pragmatism and of efficiency, they accept the necessity of expertise in carrying out research, leaving decision-making on technical matters to the experts rather than to popular consultation. The materialists doubt that those being studied either possess or can immediately acquire the skills and expertise necessary for carrying out social science research. All the research tools employed by the materialists assume a researcher who is separate from those being studied, who carries out the study, observes, and communicates the results to others. This distinction between observer and those being studied implied by objectivity is acceptable to the materialists.

Although the materialists ultimately do research to learn about the whole, they acknowledge that studying the parts tells something about the totality and that the research techniques of contemporary social science have an important role to play here. None of the research techniques of contemporary social science in the materialists' repertoire is intended to provide information directly about the whole. But the materialists argue that these research techniques do, to varying extents, provide information that can be used to describe and predict what is going on at a higher level if the person doing the research makes this a priority. Content analysis is an example of a research technique limited to an incomplete view of reality because it is restricted to the study of official documents, the written historical record, public activity that can be observed, the audiovisual record, official government statements, and so on. The materialists argue that, even if this research technique provides only low-level description, the information that results can be integrated into a broader understanding of the whole.

Because, for most, knowledge of the totality requires examining the historical dimension of a phenomenon, the materialists sometimes attempt to incorporate historical variables into the research tools of contemporary social science. Including contextual variables on individual activity also makes social surveys more relevant for the totality.

The materialists contend that the research techniques they employ are of use in obtaining objective information about reality and in distinguishing between reality and how one would like it to be (Stavenhagen, 1971:2375). For example, with respect to interviews and questionnaires, they assume that attitudes cease to be metaphysical in the sense of belonging exclusively to the realm of ideas when they are expressed and registered on a questionnaire. Some of the materialists, such as Stanislav Ossowski, go so far as to hold that, once elicited, attitudes take on a material existence and become objective social facts (Ossowski, 1962:322). According to the materialists, questionnaires provide information that can be used to change social reality. They regard qualitative research materials, such as diaries and historical documents, as authentic reflections of social reality rather than, as the philosophic Marxists contend, subjective creations.

The research techniques employed by the materialists conform to their methodological assumptions concerning observation and data. These Marxists choose research tools that acknowledge it is possible to observe, directly or indirectly, what is going on in the external world. As we saw in Chapter 3, they argue that the goal of research is to go beyond the evident, to bring out what is not immediately apparent. Most research techniques in the materialists' repertoire do, in fact, purport to go beyond appearances in the sense that they provide information that could be employed by an astute researcher in drawing non-obvious conclusions. Although the research techniques do not themselves do this, they are useful, if they permit the researcher to use the information obtained for this purpose. Several of the research techniques used by the materialists have this kind of utility: small group techniques, sociometry, social distance rating scales, and so on. They all attempt to provide information permitting the researcher to uncover deeper interpersonal relationships, to detect who is the center of social activity, the most isolated individual in a group, and so on. Systematic content analysis proposes to uncover the true meaning in a written or oral communication, to strip away the irrelevant verbiage, and to reveal non-obvious, latent meaning, which is not always apparent because of the amount of secondary information present or because of the formal presentation of the message. Judgments on the hidden content are based on a systematic, often quantitative, analysis of the manifest content. Research techniques such as field studies, life histories, and surveys often provide information that permits a description adequate for constructing non-obvious theories. The data they accumulate are usually related to what is directly observed. For example, surveys characterize reality with the aid of interviews and questionnaires. Structured observation of small group interaction describes what is manifestly observed rather than the motivation provoking behavior or discussion. But the careful researcher can construct indirect measures of underlying phenomena, analyze data, and come to conclusions that go beyond the evident.

Many of the research techniques of contemporary social science which the materialists adopt are structured as if what was being studied could be explained adequately with causal explanatory forms, completely neglecting dialectical explanation. This, of course, does not trouble those materialist Marxists who dismiss the importance of dialectical explanation in any case. But research tools such as causal modeling present problems for those materialists who retain the dialectic in a concrete form, even though they define it almost as a type of complex, causal structure. This is because causal modeling in its simplest form is incompatible with dialectical explanation. It obliges the researcher to choose from among a number of competing theories. It is not possible to prove one model "true" and others "false." Many models may "fit the data." Causal modeling only permits the researcher to indicate which of a number of competing alternative models is most appropriate for a particular set of data. Inadequate models can be eliminated, and better models, which account for more of the variance, are always possible (Blalock, 1968:159). Ultimately, if one is pragmatic about it, any choice among different models must be tested in action or judged on the basis of its performance relative to purpose.

Important steps are being taken to make causal modeling more compatible with the materialists' concrete dialectic. These advances could potentially deal with some of the limitations inherent in causal analysis, which would make it possible to consider much more complicated causal explanatory forms of symmetrical causation, feedback, and interaction (Heise, 1970; Asher, 1976). If realized, this could move causal analysis toward the study of dynamic processes that are not very different from the concrete dialectic.

Some materialists who argue that causal modeling, as it stands, is not directly dialectical have nevertheless found ways to use it in its present form so that it is consistent with their assumptions about inquiry. They suggest that causal modeling involves untangling a dialectical pattern momentarily for heuristic purposes (Marquit, 1977:171–79). A dialectical reality is broken into causal components; it is simplified. Later more variables are reintroduced, one at a time, to achieve an increasingly adequate representation of reality that ultimately is dialectical and can be applied and tested.

Many materialists are optimistic about the possibility of employing other research techniques of contemporary social science to deal with change and dialectical explanation. They argue that the information gained from most modern social science research techniques, such as surveys, content analysis, and laboratory experiments, though limited to single-point-in-time studies, can provide information to support a dialectical explanation as long as the research tool itself does not deny the possibility of a dynamic analysis. They justify their use of these techniques by arguing that, whereas these research techniques cannot directly provide dialectical explanation, they do produce results that can be worked into a dialectical explanation.

Certain modifications in the way the research techniques of contemporary social science are employed can enhance their value for dialectical explanation. Repeated measures or comparisons at different points in time can be used to study change, though this device would not satisfy all materialists seeking a dialectical form of explanation. Content analysis, for example, can be undertaken at various intervals in order to trace changes. Sociometric tests may be administered to the same group at periodic intervals to measure changes in leadership, evolution of group consensus, and the like. These changes could be correlated with other phenomena to account for observed modifications. Longitudinal data on the national economic and political characteristics of some countries offer a data base of considerable proportions for studying patterns of change pertinent for dialectical explanation. Repeating opinion polls and surveys at different points in time provides a useful, though imperfect, assessment of dialectical change. Panel analysis and time series studies offer incremental improvements in what can generally be learned from other research tools.

The materialists who emphasize dialectical explanatory forms cannot utilize all modern social science research techniques, even in modified form. A few simply do not provide information required for such explanation. Robert Bales' (1950) structured observation of small group interaction (Interaction Process Analysis) is one such research technique. Its internal coding scheme of categories is hostile to dialectical explanation because it implies that conflict is detrimental while harmony and consensus are constructive. It assumes that conflict is negative and is to be avoided. Creating group solidarity, releasing tension, and manifesting agreement are all viewed as positive forms of participation. Interventions showing disagreement, tension, or antagonism are categorized as negative contributions rather than as sources of change. The information which this research technique provides is almost impossible to incorporate into a Marxist frame of analysis where the dialectic assumes conflict to be a force for change and progress.

The materialists have a realistic view of science as potentially liberating and as free of political or class bias. This means that they accept the research strategies of modern social science with an awareness of the limitations involved. They accept that research should be independent of class or political influence. Quantitative research techniques, empirically constrained qualitative research techniques, and mathematics and statistics employed in the study of human behavior are all understood to involve the simplification of reality, not its duplication. The theories resulting from research are understood to be valid only under certain conditions and of little use without testing against purpose. If they don't work, they are of no value.

## SUMMARY

The philosophics reject the research strategy of contemporary social science and the research techniques common to it because they disagree with the assumptions underlying these research tools concerning epistemology, method, and science. They conclude that the following research techniques are useless: social surveys, structured interviews, public opinion polls, sociometric methods, quantitative content analysis, laboratory experiments, naturally occurring experiments, and data analysis techniques such as causal modeling and analysis of variance.

Those among the philosophic Marxists who do research choose qualitative, subjective research strategies such as hermeneutics, symbolic interactionism, and ethnomethodology, which have underlying assumptions in line with their own. Research techniques commonly associated with these research strategies include participant observation, field work, certain types of case studies, life history (oral biography), qualitative content analysis, unstructured, open-ended questionnaires, and in-depth interviews. As employed by the philosophics, these research tools are more idealist than materialist, more voluntarist than determinist, more subjectivist than objectivist, and more oriented toward the whole than the parts. These research techniques do not conform to the methodological requirements of contemporary social science but are in accord with the philosophics' subjective, interpretative methodological options which emphasize dialectical explanation. They fit comfortably into the philosophics' understanding of science as class-relative and fused with the political. A research technique acceptable to many philosophics, action research or participatory research, is an example of how some philosophics do research.

The deductivists do research as a form of textual exegesis or historical analysis in conformity with dialectical and historical materialism and the writings of the founders of Marxism. Although they reject contemporary social science research coming from the West and disagree with most of its assumptions, in recent years they have come to appreciate its value, especially for policymaking. As a result, they selectively cite research results from contemporary social science, ignoring those that disagree with their views and using, as a sort of legitimation, those that are in accord with their conclusions. When they undertake research along the lines of the generally accepted model, they often distort it. Research results are imposed beforehand, and the research is carried out only to illustrate the truth of the predetermined conclusions. The deductivists also have attempted to modify and use certain social science research techniques coming from the West such as systems analysis. As they employ it, systems analysis is a highly abstract, theoretical research tool that avoids focusing on concrete reality. Because it is so flexible and ill-defined, it is easily made subservient to the deductivists' political goals and is employed in regime consolidation. Deductivist research in all of its various forms outlined here is equally unsatisfactory in that it fails to measure up to the norms of contemporary social science and would be of little use in policymaking.

The structuralists divide into two groups when it comes to actually doing research. One group, which remains faithful to an Althusserian point of view, does not question his assumptions about inquiry, rejects contemporary social science research, and substitutes research tools such as discourse analysis, defined as an intellectualized, abstract form of content analysis. This research technique is reputed to be of use in studying what is left out of a written text (the invisible rather than what can be observed directly). The information that results from such abstract discourse analysis is, however, of dubious value for producing knowledge acceptable in terms of the generally accepted model of research.

Another group of structuralists rejects those elements of Althusser's assumptions about inquiry which are inconsistent with the generally accepted model and simply goes about research according to the norms of contemporary social science. The results they produce are recognized as competent by many who would not define themselves as Marxists or as structuralists.

Among the Marxists the materialists come closest to doing research acceptable in terms of contemporary social science. They adopt the same research strategies and research techniques as modern non-Marxist social scientists, emphasizing statistics, quantitative research techniques, and those qualitative research techniques based on observable experience. They are in agreement with the assumptions associated with these research tools: determinism, the goal of objectivity, direct or indirect observation of reality with empirically constrained methods, attempting to construct and test theories based on evidence.

# 6.

# KNOWLEDGE CLAIMS AND POLICYMAKING: THE VALUE OF MARXIST RESEARCH

The value of Marxist research is judged here on the basis of whether or not the results that accrue from it can (1) be used to support knowledge claims in a defensible manner and (2) be employed in formulating policy to solve real world problems. Little is gained from research if it is an end in itself and of no real value in meeting these two goals.

With regard to the first case, the value of Marxist research results is greater if they can be employed as evidence to support knowledge claims. At the same time Marxist knowledge claims are strengthened by reference to such evidence from research, though ultimately such claims are even more convincing when tested against purpose.

In the second case, to be of value Marxist research results should also be of use in producing reasoned policy based on linking the normative to the empirical so as to permit action on real world problems with a goal of improving the human condition. This is a pragmatic humanist criterion for judging the worth of research. No assumption is made that basic research is inferior to applied forms of inquiry. But both, according to this view, should ultimately be relevant for satisfying human needs, directly or indirectly.

## KNOWLEDGE CLAIMS AND RESEARCH

Marxists like everyone else are concerned with the acceptability of their knowledge claims, and their research results have a role to play here. Knowledge claims are statements of a general character which relate to the world around us. How to convince others as to the validity of one's knowledge claims is a central concern for if they are weakly defended or are argued in an unconvincing manner no one other than their author will give them any credence. Research results are one basis, though not the only, for defending knowledge claims. But those who ground their knowledge claims on evidence gained from research, recognized in terms of the generally accepted model, are more likely to find their statements of this nature taken seriously beyond their own circle. This section reveals that the materialist Marxists and the structuralists (who abandon Althusser) employ research results as a form of evidence in defending knowledge claims. This does not mean, however, that every statement they make of this order is grounded in such evidence.

### The Philosophics: Moral, Ethical Argument

Only the most fragile connection exists between the philosophics' research and knowledge claims. Because of the way they carry out inquiry and because of the goals they assign to it, the link between research results and knowledge claims is weakened. Their knowledge claims are often phrased in global moral terms, and the pertinence of research for statements at this level often escapes them. In most cases they simply abandon any possibility of using research results as a basis of support for their knowledge claims.

The philosophics do not produce research that conforms to the requirements of the generally accepted model, and it is, therefore, of little use in supporting broader knowledge claims. As was shown above, when the philosophics undertake inquiry they employ subjective and qualitative research strategies and research techniques. They exaggerate the importance for research of individual experience defined in classical idealist terms, as extremely personal and unique.

The goals which the philosophics set for the research process are so political and personal that research becomes a goal in and of itself independent of any role it might have in terms of evidence to defend knowledge claims. As seen in Chapter 5, many of these Marxists see it as a way to achieve personal truth rather than as an effort to discover something more general about reality. It is a participatory activity, a form of human development and consciousness-raising, a justification for social animation. For the philosophics who do this kind of research, inquiry is part of a larger process of human emancipation, seeking to make sense of a world which, before being experienced in this manner of research, was merely alien.

The philosophic Marxists' knowledge claims are expressed in terms of general, universal principles, primarily of an ethical nature, and are seldom defined with reference to research. For example, Marx's communism, without any appeal to evidence, is said to provide the social arrangements where "the whole range of human conduct and relations would become expressions of man's true being..., and man would find that true and ultimate freedom which is the necessary destiny of man" (Kamenka, 1966:119). The philosophics justify their knowledge claims in much the same way as they construct theory (discussed in Chapter 3)—in terms of moral argument, righteousness, or political priorities expressed as purity of a class perspective (Meszaros, 1972). For example, one philosophic Marxist claims that "in an alienated society apersonal factors determine what man is and what he can become." People are said to be "slaves to a dead material," that is, *money*, which is the "most abstract of these factors." Money, the author tells us, destroys relations between people; "friendship and love lose all connection with the personality of the partners." We are told that "Marx's model of man is a moral model," that money involves the commercialization of human relations, and that people must "cease letting money and other material factors determine mutual human relations" (Fritzhand, 1966:178-79). Certainly money may be the principle source of human oppression and corruption but the author assumes this to be so and argues from an ethical perspective with no reference to research or any other form of observable experience. As a consequence of this kind of analysis the philosophics are unable to distinguish argument from evidence and their knowledge claims are not very convincing to non-Marxists who do not share their assumptions about the world or about research.

## The Deductivists: The Writings of the Founders

The deductivists argue that their claims to knowledge are based on research. They attempt to defend them in two ways. First, and most importantly, knowledge claims are said to be true because they accord with classic forms of deductivist research which involves textual exegesis of Marxist writings and the doctrines of historical and dialectical materialism. Second, the deductivists selectively refer to research undertaken in terms of the generally accepted model. But as will be seen, in both cases, the kind of evidence they provide is very weak, and unlikely to be generally recognized as valid by many outside their own circles.

In the first case, the deductivists are unsuccessful in their attempts to defend their knowledge claims on the basis of their own "research" based on textual exegesis or, in more recent years, on Western research strategies modified for use in the USSR such as abstract systems analysis. Research, the way they define it, in terms of textual consistency, is limited to "prove and demonstrate." It is a deductive process wherein prediction becomes prophecy because it is made on the basis of theory alone and is not supported by evidence. For example, Stalin held that poverty and unemployment disappeared under socialism as Marx had predicted, and so as early as the 1930s he denied it existed in the USSR but without any reference to evidence. In the mid–1960s research by materialist Marxists in that same country revealed that the situation was very different from what Stalin had assumed. Although Soviet families were better off in the 1960s than had been the case thirty years earlier, one-third of the households sampled had less than the minimum necessary income and were found to be "underprovisioned" (Matthews, 1978:19–20).

Examples of how deductivists defend their knowledge claims can be found in the journal called *Social Sciences* published starting in the early 1970s by the Soviet Academy of Sciences. Each number contains articles that explain the "correct" view as set down by Marx, Engels, Lenin, or the Communist Party of the Soviet Union on topics relevant for social science. These articles often begin and end with a quotation from Marx or Lenin. Changes in observed phenomena are said to have been foreseen by the founders of Marxism. The vast majority of citations and footnotes refer to Marx, Lenin, or Engels. (For an especially good example see Fedoseyev, 1983.) Any effort to defend knowledge claims on the basis of the deductivists' "research" is contradictory. When no evidence exists on which to base their knowledge claims, they assert them dogmatically arguing they are consistent with the writings of the founders of Marxism.

The deductivists fail to distinguish between weighing evidence and illustrating a position when they attempt to defend their knowledge claims with the selective use of research from studies done in the West and considered acceptable in terms of contemporary social science. They accept the results of research from the West when, on occasion, they find evidence for a particular point with which they agree. The pertinence of research results from the same sources which call into question points essential to their knowledge claims are ignored or criticized. Equally important problems arise when evidence for defending knowledge claims comes from a research project whose results were determined in advance. Here "findings" hardly constitute evidence at all. The way the deductivists employ systems analysis, abstractly without reference to data, makes it almost irrelevant to their knowledge claims.

Ultimately, for the deductivists, knowledge is true because it corresponds to the premises in the writings of the founders. Any research evidence used to support knowledge claims cannot conflict with these sources. Conclusions are assumed to follow logically and automatically without contradiction from textual exegesis. Understandably, knowledge claims so defended are of little interest to those who do not share the deductivists' particular Marxist orientation.

### The Althusserian Structuralists: Coherent Theory Is Sufficient

Those structuralists who remain faithful to Althusser relate their research to their knowledge claims, but both their definition of knowledge claims and their refusal to test conclusions arising from research make it unlikely that the results will be of interest outside Althusser's own circle of followers.

For the Althusserian structuralists knowledge claims are justified by reference to theories unrelated to the real world. According to Althusser, knowledge is "an intellectual construct, not a receptacle of the imprints of what lies outside it" (Benton, 1984:38). Knowledge results from theoretical practice or a form of production defined as a kind of intellectual work that makes its own raw materials, for example, concepts, principles, and laws. Intellectual labor alone produces new concepts and principles. Knowledge is grounded in theory that is judged only on the character of its intellectual structure, on its "comprehensiveness, or its lack of contradictions, or with respect to its thought structures alone" (Binns, 1973).

The results of discourse analysis, a research strategy acceptable to many Althusserian structuralists, provides an example of how the structuralists defend their knowledge claims. While coherent, consistent, logical, and of interest, these results make little reference to empirical reality and are never tested except intuitively. Logic, consistency, and other internal characteristics of theory are a requirement of all knowledge, but they are not by themselves sufficient for everyone. Because Althusser's logic and symbols do not make reference to what takes place in the real world in terms of evidence that is testable and can be applied, non-Marxists requiring such a link are not likely to accept his knowledge claims.

## The Materialists and the Non-Althusserian Structuralists Say Research Is a Form of Evidence and Can Be Used to Defend Knowledge Claims

Both the materialist Marxists and the structuralists who have abandoned Althusser's assumptions about inquiry defend their knowledge claims with reference to research results assumed to constitute a form of evidence. Both groups undertake research in terms close to those of contemporary social science. They view research as one way to learn about what is going on in reality. Research results are understood to be of use in defending knowledge claims because they have been tested. This increases the legitimacy of their knowledge claims in the eyes of many non-Marxists.

Examples of how the materialists in the USSR have used research results to defend their knowledge claims during periods when the government permitted inquiry along the lines of the generally accepted model can be found in journals of translated articles such as those in *Soviet Sociology* from the early 1960s through the early 1970s. English-language summaries of research published only in Russian are available (Weinberg, 1974; Matthews, 1978), and they, too, indicate the attempts of these materialist Marxists to link knowledge claims to results of defensible research.

Jean Lojkine and Ralph Miliband are two examples of materialist Marxists from Western countries who defend their knowledge claims with research results. Miliband argues in *The State in Capitalist Society* that private economic power continues to exist in advanced capitalist societies, that it is ever more concentrated as time goes on, and that it has preponderant influence on state policy and action (Miliband, 1969). He uses research results from surveys, government and private statistical data banks, and the like, to defend this claim. Lojkine in France argues that urban social problems are in part due to the united action of the French capitalist state, the large industrial groups and finance capital, in that they mold territorial space in cities according to class interests. Statistics and secondary data from a variety of sources are brought to bear on this point (Lojkine, 1977).

The work of Erik Olin Wright offers an example of a structuralist who abandoned Althusser and has proceeded with inquiry along the lines of contemporary social science norms, using research results to defend his knowledge claims. For example, employing data from national social surveys in the United States, he argues that class "defined as positions within the social relations of production, plays a central role in mediating income inequality in capitalist society" (Wright, 1979).

### Summary

The materialists and the non-Althusserian structuralists defend their knowledge claims in terms familiar to modern social science with reference to research assumed to provide one form of evidence. The philosophics reject this view completely, considering research superficial to their knowledge claims. They separate the two, assigning different political and personal goals to research and defending their knowledge claims on the basis of ethics and morality, or the superiority of a particular class perspective. The deductivists state that their knowledge claims are based on research, but this assertion means little because their research is not generally recognized as valid by many outside their own circle. The deductivists end up defending their knowledge claims principally with reference to the writings of the founders of Marxism. Although they make use of social science research results in an effort to support their knowledge claims, it is either biased in the way it is selected or limited because it is carried out with conclusions set down in advance. Althusserian structuralists make knowledge claims unrelated to the real world. They support them without reference to concrete reality or evidence but exclusively on the basis of the logic and coherence of the theory to which it refers.

## LINKING THE EMPIRICAL AND THE NORMATIVE TO PRODUCE POLICY

We turn now to an even more rigorous requirement for Marxist research, namely, that posed by the policymaking model. If the research and knowledge which Marxists produce are to be of value, they must contribute to real world action in the sense of being useful as a basis for solving problems and constructing policies that will improve the human condition. The goal here is not to evaluate the specific social, economic, and political policies of the various Marxist currents. Rather, it is to determine which of them has the ability to produce the rules of action required by the policymaking model briefly outlined in Chapter 1 and explained in more detail below.

The task of assessing whether Marxist research is of value in policymaking requires a detour to examine how Marxists view ethical matters because policymaking involves both normative and empirical dimensions. In policymaking, normative structures or priorities (value positions) are combined with empirical instruments that are at least partly constructed from research in order to yield policies assessed on their ability to give preferred results (Meehan, 1981).

Policymaking, as defined here, whether by Marxists or non-Marxists, involves a number of steps, based on both normative and empirical instruments of choice. First, Marxists interested in policymaking must generate projections of possible outcomes. A selection is then made from among these alternatives on the basis of the impact of the proposed policy on the human condition. Next, the preference decided on must be justified. Finally, an action program for achieving the chosen option must be set forth (Meehan, 1981).

Until now we have looked at Marxist research based on evidence relevant for constructing only the empirical instruments necessary for policymaking. We have seen that, for the most part, it is the materialists and some of the structuralists (those who have abandoned Althusser) who undertake research such that it would be possible for them to produce these tools. In this section our focus expands to include normative instruments and policymaking itself.

It is not the intention of all Marxist groups to produce policy, but the question here is whether what they do, when they do research and come to normative positions, can be used in reasoned policymaking. If it can, the policies that result are likely to be of value to a broader non-Marxist audience.

If policies are guides to action, Marxists seeking to costruct policies must attempt to produce both the empirical and the normative instruments that go into the formulation of an action program. *Empirical instruments* in terms of the policymaking model result from research and consist of a theory that indicates the range of alternatives from which a choice must be made. The goal of these empirical tools is to point to the consequences arising from each available line of action and to outline a strategy for attaining the preferred outcome; they are necessarily predictive, requiring a causal relation to permit intervention. The policymaking model's *normative instruments* rank priorities or preferences. They involve weighing, comparing, and ranking different known alternatives or outcomes in terms of past experience and assigning priorities to each on the basis of their respective consequences for the conditions of human life. These normative tools are constructed with the same basic method as the empirical instruments in the sense that both consist of systematic generalization of organized patterns of observable experience in specific situations (Meehan, 1981:Chapters 5 and 6; Meehan, 1982, Chapter 3).

This view of policymaking assumes that the empirical and the normative are neither completely distinct nor inseparably fused. Normative aspects of policy formation are tied to the quality of the empirical knowledge available. The adequacy of the empirical instruments is dependent on their capacity to fulfill normative requirements. Both the normative tools and the empirical instrument that go into policymaking are tested through concrete application and are evaluated in relation to available alternatives. Ultimately, policy choices involve finding not the best policy, but that which is relatively superior to the others.

Most Marxists, with the exception of the structuralists, consider the normative to be pertinent for policymaking. Their inclination to give priority to improving the human condition was present within Marxism from the beginning. They are preoccupied with the ethical and its role in policymaking, that is, they acknowledge that the normative has a legitimate role in the process of choosing among alternative policies. They consider the normative to be central to decision-making, demanding political commitment in an almost inescapable manner. From a logical point of view, this should encourage Marxists to link the normative to the empirical to produce policies, though not all of the Marxists do so.

Marxists who have held office and have assumed administrative responsibility should, at least in theory, be more sensitive to the importance of producing reasoned policy than those Marxists who have not shared this governing experience. We will see that, as with theory construction and application discussed in Chapter 3, holding office is a necessary but not sufficient condition for encouraging Marxists to focus attention on reasoned policymaking.

Previewing the discussion in this section, we will see that the research produced by the materialists plays a central role in their efforts at policymaking. As a result, the materialist Marxists actually have the capacity to link the normative to the empirical and to produce reasoned policy that is of concrete utility in terms of improving the human condition. The philosophics do not have the tools to produce the basis for reasoned action. In any case they are suspicious of the value of policymaking in general for political reasons. Not much use can be made of the knowledge produced by the structuralists either. They give little attention to policymaking, deny the importance of the normative, and have a view of reality as structural, which makes policymaking meaningless. Although the deductivists attempt to link empirical instruments based on research (as they define it and carry it out) to normative instruments, the results are disappointing because their policy choices are not based on a comparison of possible outcomes of the various options available.

## The Philosophics Emphasize the Normative Without the Empirical

The philosophic Marxists have normative views that guide action, but these are not linked to empirical instruments so that reasoned policy results. Among the Marxists they are most dedicated to the principle of satisfying human needs. They emphasize the value of human life, stressing the importance of the individual rather than the collective. They express their normative preferences as general moral convictions or broad ethical propositions. This was illustrated in the discussion concerning how they defend their knowledge claims. Their normative judgments are not tentative or situational but absolute; they strive for the ideal outcome rather than the best possible outcome in any situation. This makes it very difficult to produce effective corrigible policies. In any case they have serious reservations about the political implications of policymaking.

Why is it so difficult for the philosophics to systematically link their normative concerns to empirical outcomes so as to provide the basis for action in the form of defensible policy? First, as we saw in Chapter 5, they cannot and do not produce the empirical instruments required for policymaking. These Marxists make assumptions about inquiry which are incompatible with the norms of contemporary social sciences. They criticize those Marxists who do research in line with the generally accepted model and deny the value of their results. As a consequence, the philosophics cannot improve policy on the basis of experience in the form of organized data gathering. Second, the philosophics reject the idea that empirical research results can be related to normative choice structures because they say that the normative is contaminated by any attempt to link it to systematic description and science. As a result, the policy positions advanced by the philosophics cannot be supported systematically since their normative views are never evaluated in terms of success or failure of application. This leads to a relativist position in which there is no basis for claiming one normative choice is better than any other because the consequences of a particular choice remain unknown. Third, because of their understanding of science (as subservient to politics and class), they fuse the normative and the empirical by politicizing the research process itself. From the point of view of the policymaking model, it is perfectly appropriate for political options to be constituent elements of the normative instruments on which reasoned argument relevant for action is based. But refusing to treat the initial construction of empirical and normative instruments as separate projects leads to considerable confusion and jeopardizes the quality of both these essential tools of policymaking. In sum, the philosophics do not have the tools to make decisions by comparing possible outcomes.

Some of the philosophic Marxists have politically based objections to any effort at policymaking. Using research results in decision-making, they say, assumes that change can be predicted and controlled. For the philosophics this is deterministic and oppressive because (1) it encourages "social engineering" in the hands of planners and administrators, (2) it leads to "liberal policy directives," (3) it promotes reformism, and (4) it ultimately lowers the political consciousness of workers (Heiple and Pozzuto, 1975:14). According to these philosophics, the use of research results, especially in the production of theory relevant for constructing the empirical instruments required for policymaking, can have literally catastrophic results that do irreparable harm (Gramsci, 1971:428–29). This is because any transformation of reality leading to human emancipation, individual growth, and personal development must, as they see it, be freely chosen and undertaken by conscious individuals, through personal struggle, and not imposed by outside policymakers who are merely uncaring, external authorities.

In general, philosophics do not give much importance to producing effective, reasoned policy as a means to satisfying human needs. In part, this is because they have seldom held positions of authority in the past and are unlikely to do so in the near future. In addition, many of them propose that the human condition can be improved only by dramatic political action in the form of revolution. Revolutions cannot by definition be implemented in the manner of reasoned policy.

When philosophical Marxists have successfully organized revolutions, their policy choices, formulated in absolute terms, have flowed directly from their ideals and their aspirations without an assessment of whether or not their goals were achievable within the limits of human capacity. When thrust into positions of authority, when confronted with the constraints of governing, policymaking, and administration for any reasonable length of time, many philosophics seem to lean toward the more pragmatic materialist Marxist orientation. For example, in the case of the USSR those who carried out the revolution were romantics, what I call here philosophic Marxists. They moved to socialize the economy with dramatic nationalizations almost immediately. Similarly idealistic policies were established in the areas of social policy. Later, in 1921, Lenin reversed himself as performance became more important than political principle in policymaking; private trade was reestablished, and capitalist economic forms were restored in what was called the New Economic Policy. Many other revolutions have experienced this type of evolution in orientation from romantic to pragmatic, from philosophic to materialist Marxism.

### The Structuralists Say Policy Is Not Important and the Normative Is Irrelevant

Few structuralists are interested in policymaking, and in any case it would be nearly impossible for them to link the empirical to the normative and produce policy. First, they emphasize theory but dismiss any need or possibility of producing it on the basis of observable evidence. As was observed in assessing their assumptions about inquiry, the structuralists understand research to take place strictly in the realm of the intellect, independent of evidence. Second, the structuralists deny altogether the importance of the normative which they say is merely ideology and closely associated with humanism because it implies the acceptance of empiricism and idealism. For the structuralists, humanism attributes a universal essence to human beings and expresses this as a characteristic of each individual, therefore detracting attention from structures. Because the normative often emphasizes personal freedom, they argue that it is opposed to science and a class analysis (Blackburn and Jones, 1972:368). Consequently, they see little use in linking the empirical and the normative to formulate policies.

Third, it is difficult for the structuralists to produce knowledge useful for policymaking because they see reality in terms of abstract amorphous structures and attribute little importance to the role of individual actors. Policy implies specific actions and identifiable actors capable of initiating change. The structures which these

Marxists seek to uncover constitute a reality beyond the power of any individual person to modify. As the structuralists see it, no specific actor can be held responsible for any precise concrete action. Their structural determinism and their structural causality leave no room for attributing responsibility to exact sources of influence. Within their view it is difficult to isolate the source of a problem or to point out any precise way to change an undesirable situation. Policy has no meaning in such a world.

The structuralists who abandoned Althusser ignore his requirements for research and undertake inquiry in terms of the generally accepted model, but they are only slightly more likely than those who retain all of his assumptions about inquiry to produce reasoned policy. The non-Althusserian structuralists have difficulty producing policy in the terms defined here because they do not link the empirical instruments (which they are capable of constructing) to a structured set of normative choices. This is because they never abandon Althusser's view that the normative is irrelevant. Few structuralists, either those who agree with Althusser or those who oppose his views on how to do research, have ever held political office or have had any need for policymaking tools. This, too, reduces the likelihood of their producing policy valuable for decision-making.

### The Deductivists Use Rule Ethics to Construct Normative Instruments and to Produce Policy of Dubious Quality

The deductivists do not produce knowledge useful for action, intervention, and policymaking. Although they link the normative to the empirical, the quality of the elements involved is dubious and the whole process takes place in a milieu divorced from concrete reality. As indicated in Chapter 5, the deductivists' assumptions about research diverge radically from the norms required by contemporary social science. This means they cannot produce defensible empirical instruments as required for reasoned policy. They arrive at their normative choices on the basis of a rule ethic rather than a consequential ethic. Therefore, their normative choices are made on the basis of the rules of dialectical materialism and historical materialism rather than by comparing the consequences of various normative and empirical outcomes. They accept the policies produced by this process because they result from use of the approved method. "It is with Marx, Engels, and Lenin that C. P. S. U. [the Communist Party of the USSR] checks every step it takes" (Andropov, 1984:23). They do not judge policy in terms of how it actually influences human lives and situations, or on the basis of whether or not it actually succeeds in reaching intended goals but rather on the basis of its conformity to the pre-given rules, as part of the process of the "struggle" for the "purity" of Marxist-Leninist principles (Andropov, 1984:7, 24). Given this constraint, the deductivists, in general, cannot measure their policies against reality, and, therefore, they do not learn from their own mistakes and make an effort to improve performance on the basis of experience.

From the deductivists we also learn that holding office and having the institutional capacity to implement one's policies is not sufficient, in itself, to produce reasoned policy. Although they have frequently been in power, the quality of their research and their normative instruments of choice make it very difficult for them to produce policies that work and are convincing to others. When decision-making takes place in the absence of any adequate description of reality, without the tools of reasoned policy, a plan of action may be refused even when it is recognized to be necessary. On the other hand, dramatic policy changes may be initiated without prior analysis or study of the consequences. Examples of their administrative inefficiency abound. In the USSR under Stalin, the deductivists accepted and implemented T. D. Lysenko's policies in the fields of genetics and agriculture, though these policies were not adequately tested and repeatedly failed to produce the desired or expected results; they did so simply because the policies he advocated followed logically from the accepted doctrine (Medvedev, 1969:22–37; Lecourt, 1977:Chapters 4 and 5). In China during the Cultural Revolution, the results of the deductivists' policymaking process were equally disastrous (Lewin, 1974:116). The general consensus today is that these programs produced outcomes that ignored human consequences, with monstrous results.

In some historical situations, during severe social, political, and economic crises, the deductivists have attempted to define empirical instruments and have systematically considered normative options to produce policy that was subsequently revised on the basis of experience. But only in exceptional circumstances have the deductivists been willing to put dogma aside and let the evidence decide the issue.

## The Materialists Use Consequential Ethics to Construct Normative Instruments and Produce Reasoned Policy

The materialists have the potential to generate the kinds of tools that reasoned policy requires, that is, relating empirical outcomes to normative instruments in ways that permit reasoned intervention, action, and policymaking. Chapter 5 demonstrated how these Marxists tend to produce research in line with the norms of contemporary social science. This makes it possible for them to construct the empirical instruments (imperfect though they may be) needed for policymaking. Materialists are more interested than the other Marxists in producing causal theory which is required for reasoned policy. They test research results against evidence and obtain information for refining policy by applying it.

The materialists formulate their normative instruments in terms of consequential ethics. In other words, they make normative choices on the basis of consequences for human populations. In establishing normative priorities, the materialists emphasize collective human welfare over the interests of the individual. Their policies are aimed at increasing production or at efficiency which, at least theoretically, is supposed to improve general life conditions and satisfy human needs with increasing effectiveness. For pragmatic reasons their normative choices result from a comparison of various possible outcomes given their formal goals.

Historically, the materialists have produced policies that have been tested in concrete circumstances and modified or abandoned on the basis of feedback from application. The materialists have a reputation of sacrificing Marxist dogma for results in the policymaking process. For example, in both Cuba and China today these Marxists have increasingly come to depend on material rather than moral incentives to increase production because the material incentives have been found to be more effective. This often requires that they compromise their commitment to socialist-Communist economic institutional forms. There are indications that in the USSR feedback mechanisms were employed in the field of administration even when this required certain modifications in the role of the Communist Party in decision-making (Schwartz, 1973:261–62).

Research by Soviet sociologists appears to have had an impact on social policy in the USSR, at least during the periods when the materialists held power (Hahn, 1977). An example illustrates the policy implications of materialist Marxist research and the potential use of this kind of inquiry for policy formulation in socialist countries. A. G. Zdravomyslov and V. A. Iadov first provide the normative instruments for policymaking in that they assume that a higher standard of living is better than a lower level (1966). Next, their empirical instruments lead them to conclude that satisfied workers are more productive than dissatisfied workers. Their study of the attitudes and productivity of young workers in Leningrad indicates that worker satisfaction can be increased by encouraging workers to use their "intellectual ability in carrying out the job, by improving the material work conditions themselves and by structuring the environment," so that the individual has the opportunity to improve his or her skills on the job. They conclude that making an exclusively "verbal approach" (on the basis of ideology) to achieve worker satisfaction is fruitless.

Finally, an example of materialist Marxists making policy in the Third World involves the field of agricultural policy in Nicaragua just after the overthrow of Anastasio Somoza Debayle. Land belonging to the dictator's family was confiscated in July 1979, and state farms were set up. Peasants were hired and paid a salary to work on these farms as employees. The goal was political, that is, to transform peasants into workers and thus raise their class consciousness and build urban-rural solidarity. When studies showed agricultural productivity falling off, the pragmatic materialists among the Sandinistas prevailed and a new policy was implemented, designed to increase output. Hence land was distributed directly to individual peasants or to private peasant cooperatives, even though this had the political effect of maintaining a capitalist form of agricultural production (Vaillancourt, 1986; Collins, 1982).

The materialists' experience in political office has encouraged them to produce reasoned policy. They have frequently been elected or appointed to important political posts, and have participated in governing in the socialist countries, in the West (as member of parliamentary-oriented Communist parties, as partners in coalition governments, and independently on the municipal level political scene), and in Third World countries. As a result, they have frequently found themselves with the institutional arrangements that permit policymaking in line with their priorities. This has allowed them to test policy in action and to revise it when necessary. They are pragmatic and are generally willing to settle for the best policy among a limited number of alternatives rather than insisting on a search for the "best" policy.

The fact that the materialists (1) have the intellectual tools to build empirical instruments (2) are able to produce the normative structures for making choices, and (3) can potentially link the two to produce policy is no guarantee that they have actually produced reasoned policy in the past or any assurance that they will do so in the future. It is merely a statement of their greater potential ability to do so compared to the other Marxist groups. Despite this qualification and even though evaluations of performance in power are often complicated and sometimes politically motivated, a convincing case can be made that the materialists have taken the occasion of their terms in office to satisfy human needs and better conditions.

### Summary

With regard to which of the various Marxist currents can produce policies of use in solving real world problems by linking normative instruments (ranked priorities) and empirical instruments grounded in research results, the materialists appear to be the most successful. They have established their normative choices on the basis of consequential ethics, and they are pragmatic and judge policy with reference to purpose, that is, on its relative success in achieving defined aims (improve conditions for human populations) and on its consequence for human populations given the available alternatives.

The philosophics attribute the greatest importance to normative matters expressed as improving the human condition. They make their normative choices on the basis of Marxist humanism, but they fail to relate their normative preferences to empirical instruments and, therefore, forfeit any possibility of producing policy or intervening effectively.

The Althusserian structuralists are in the worst position among the Marxists with regard to the imperatives of policymaking. They dismiss any possibility of producing the necessary empirical tools based on the results of defensible research (those structuralists who have abandoned Althusser excepted). In addition, they associate the normative with humanism which they reject because they say it is merely ideology and implies the acceptance of empiricism and idealism. Finally, because they focus on structures defined abstractly, it is impossible for them to produce policy relevant for concrete situations where individual actions play a decisive role.

The deductivists produce policy, but it is of little interest because their empirical instruments are usually formal and are derived directly and deductively from historical and dialectical materialism. Their normative tools follow a rule ethic, that is, they are judged on the basis of their conformity to the rule rather than on the basis of success in achieving the desired goal. The policies they construct are not subject to testing and cannot be corrected in light of mistakes. Neither are they very convincing to others in the scientific community.

Holding office is a necessary condition but not a sufficient incentive for Marxists to link the empirical and the normative to produce policy that can contribute to real world action. Having had the political experience of being in power and having been required to make decisions that affect people's lives should encourage them to be sensitive to the utility of reasoned policy. The philosophics and the structuralists have seldom been in positions of authority; they do not produce reasoned policy. The deductivists and the materialists have had much more experience in holding office. Although this has encouraged the materialists to produce reasoned policy, it has had no such effect on the deductivists who generally advocate policies on the basis of whether or not they are compatible with dialectical and historical materialism.

## THE OVERALL VALUE OF MARXIST RESEARCH: A SUMMARY

What can non-Marxists expect to gain from examining Marxist research? The answer, as observed repeatedly throughout this book, is that it depends on which Marxist current is being discussed.

Many of the materialist Marxists carry out research that is of potential value to non-Marxists who agree with the central elements of what is described in Chapter 1 as the generally accepted model. These Marxists make materialist epistemological assumptions about inquiry. Their methods are empirically constrained. Their understanding of science and its relation to class and politics is consistent with the norms of modern social science. As a result, they have the tools to undertake research that is defensible in terms of the generally accepted model. When they do research, many of the materialists use research strategies and research techniques that conform closely to those of contemporary social science to describe reality. They often test results against experience and apply their research findings in the real world to obtain feedback for improving theory.

The materialists use the results of research to defend their knowledge claims. They are the only Marxist group able to provide the tools needed to link the normative to the empirical to formulate policy for intervention and action that can be used to improve the human condition. Their normative choices follow from consequential ethics which are linked to empirical instruments grounded in research. They have the capacity to construct policy of use in satisfying human needs and to evaluate it with respect to purpose, that is, on the basis of results of application.

Because of the way the materialist Marxists undertake inquiry and make policy, others can profit from what they have learned, especially about their own experiences in power and their involvement in constructing new social arrangements and institutional structures. Countries governed by Marxists today face many of the same problems that plague non-Marxist societies. Juvenile delinquency, worker alienation, and alcoholism are examples. The results of materialist Marxist research on these and other topics are of potential interest to non-Marxists.

The research results of the materialists have only a probable utility because they are so little known. Many non-Marxists in Western countries who would be interested in this research are unaware that it even exists because its diffusion has been quite limited in the West. The philosophics, who dominate Western Marxism, feel that such research is of no value, and the deductivists who controlled the Communist Party formations for so many years in the West agree. The materialists in the socialist countries have historically been discouraged from doing research when the deductivists were in power. They were oppressed directly when Stalin, a deductivist himself, was in control. The philosophic Marxists in the West have discounted the importance of the materialists' research efforts. They generally assimilate this Marxist current to that of Stalinism (what has here been called deductivist Marxism) whose research approach, as we have seen, is quite different from that of the materialists.

Non-Marxists have almost nothing to learn from the deductivists' research which is based on unacceptable assumptions about inquiry. Their method is formal and *a priori* and is dependent on dialectical and historical materialism. They criticize modern science, and they make social science subservient to politics. This group of Marxists presents a negative example of how to do research. They are hostile to inquiry in the sense in which it is recognized in the scientific community. For more productive, testable research strategies they substitute a simple textual exegesis of the writings of the founding fathers of Marxism or modified Western research techniques such as abstract systems analysis. The way they undertake inquiry does not provide a convincing basis for their knowledge claims. Sometimes the deductivists use research findings from Western sources to illustrate the correctness of their own preferred theoretical views, but this amounts to illustration rather than a serious weighing of evidence. Basing policy on research of dubious quality is a risky business and has had drastic consequences. Overall, these Marxists have made almost no contribution to the store of knowledge that has come to be identified with modern social sciences.

The failure of the deductivists to undertake research which is recognized as defensible to a broader audience, and their inability to relate their normative choices to empirical instruments based on research and other kinds of evidence, have resulted in an appalling and irretrievable loss of potential knowledge. What might have been learned from these Marxists' experiences when they held political authority and were involved in decision-making remains unknown. Certainly, the consequences of the inadequate policies which the deductivists imposed without concern for vast human populations led to tremendous suffering. But relatively little of this has been systematically studied, and so, many of the same mistakes may be made again in the future.

Neither will non-Marxists learn much from the philosophic Marxists' research. These Marxists also make assumptions about inquiry which have little in common with the generally accepted model; in many cases their views are in direct conflict with it. Their epistemological assumptions are voluntarist and idealist. Their general method is interpretative and dialectical. The philosophics reject modern science and any attempt to make their own research systematic or rigorous in this sense. They define the scientific enterprise as subjective and relative. Science itself is said to be subservient to class and politics. The philosophics fuse politics and science. This leads them to reject the research strategies of modern social science, to reorient the goal of research (toward political education, political consciousness-raising, and personal emancipation), and to substitute qualitative research strategies. In some cases they employ research techniques that allow for the active role of those being studied and that provide new forms of direct involvement for the researcher. This type of participatory research while of interest in and of itself, is of little help in supporting knowledge claims or providing defensible research results needed for reasoned policymaking.

The Althusserian structuralists produce almost no research of value to non-Marxists. Their assumptions about inquiry are a combination of views, some of which are in accord with those of contemporary social science (structural determinism, objectivity, aspects of positivism, natural science independent of politics, and rejection of a class-relative science) and others which are in complete disagreement with it (anti-empiricism and Marxism as a science). The research they produce is highly theoretical and abstract, and is of little use in defending knowledge claims in terms recognized by modern social science. The Althusserian structuralists produce neither empirical instruments based on research nor reasoned normative choices for policy designed to better the human condition.

Those structuralists who have abandoned Althusser's assumptions undertake research in terms recognized as useful with respect to the generally accepted model and produce results of significant interest to non-Marxist social scientists who agree with this view. Their research can be used as evidence for defending knowledge claims. But because they reject the importance of the normative dimension of policy formulation, they cannot provide the basis for reasoned intervention to solve problems in the real world.

The fact that the philosophics and many of the structuralists have failed to develop research strategies that are convincing to a broader audience and likely to produce reasoned policy has nowhere near the consequences that result from the deductivists' failure in this area. This is because these structuralists and philosophics have seldom held power and been in a position to make decisions that concretely affect human life. Their inability to systematically and critically conduct research on their experiences and to learn from what they have encountered does not constitute an insurmountable loss to humankind.

These conclusions do not mean that the research produced by the philosophics, deductivists, and Althusserian structuralists is without interest to non-Marxists who share certain assumptions about inquiry with these Marxists. It only means that the research they produce and their knowledge claims are not acceptable within the norm of contemporary mainstream social science or of use in terms of the policymaking model as defined here.

# BIBLIOGRAPHY

ADORNO, Theodor, et al. (1950). *The Authoritarian Personality*. New York: Harper.

ADORNO, Theodor (1969). "Du rapport entre la théorie et l' empirie en sociologie" (The relationship between theory and empiric in sociology), *L'homme et la société*, 13:127–33.

AFANASYEV, Victor (1979). "Systems Approach in Social Cognition," *Social Sciences*, 10 (1):29–44.

AGGER, Benjamin (1976). "The Uses of Marx: The Concept of Epistemology in Contemporary Marxism." Ph.D. thesis, University of Toronto.

AGGER, Benjamin (1977). "Dialectical Sensibility, I. Critical Theory, Scientism and Empiricism, II. Towards a New Intellectuality," *Canadian Journal of Political and Social Theory*, 1:3–34, 47–56.

ALEKSEEV, B. K., B. Z. Doktorov, and B. M. Firsov (1980). "The Study of Public Opinion Experience and Problems," *Soviet Sociology*, 18 (Spring):38–54.

ALLEN, V. L. (1975). *Social Analysis: A Marxist Critique and Alternative*. London: Longman.

ALTHUSSER, Louis (1965). *For Marx*. London: New Left Books.

ALTHUSSER, Louis (1971). *Lenin and Philosophy and Other Essays*. London: New Left Books.

ALTHUSSER, Louis (1972). "Reply to John Lewis (Self Criticism)," *Marxism Today*, October, 310–18, November, 343–49.

ALTHUSSER, Louis (1976a). *Essays in Self Criticism*. London: New Left Books.

ALTHUSSER, Louis (1976b). *Positions*. Paris: Editions Sociales.

ALTHUSSER, Louis (1977). "Toward Fusion," *Theoretical Review*, 1 (November-December):2–13.

ALTHUSSER, Louis, and E. Balibar (1968). *Reading Capital.* London: New Left Books.

ANDERSON, Perry (1976). *Consideration on Western Marxism.* London: New Left Books.

ANDERSON, Perry (1980). *Arguments Within English Marxism.* London: New Left Books.

ANDERSON, Perry (1984). *In the Tracks of Historical Materialism.* Chicago: University of Chicago Press.

ANDROPOV, Yuri (1984). "The Teaching of Karl Marx and Some Questions of Building Socialism in the USSR," *Social Sciences,* 15 (1):7–25.

ANIKIN, A. (1975). *A Science in Its Youth (Pre-Marxian Political Economy).* Moscow: Progress Publishers.

ANTONIO, Robert J., and Parviz Piran (1978). "The Poverty of American Sociology: Historicity and Empiricism," Livermore, Colo.: Red Feather Institute for Advanced Studies in Sociology.

APPELBAUM, Richard (1978). "Marxist Method: Structural Constraints and Social Praxis," *The American Sociologist.* 13:73–81.

APPELBAUM, Richard (1979). "Born Again Functionalism? A Reconsideration of Althusser's Structuralism," *Insurgent Sociologist.* 9 (Summer):18–33.

ASHER, Herbert (1976). *Causal Modeling, Quantitative Applications in the Social Sciences.* Beverly Hills, Calif.: Sage Publications.

BALES, Robert F. (1950). *Interaction Process Analysis.* Chicago: University of Chicago Press.

BANDYOPADHYAY, Pradeep (1971). "One Sociology or Many: Some Issues in Radical Sociology," *Sociological Review,* 19 (February):5–30.

BARAN, Paul A. (1969). *The Longer View, Essays Toward a Critique of Political Economy.* New York: Monthly Review Press.

BARTON, Allen (1971). "Empirical Methods and Radical Sociology: A Liberal Critique," in J. David Colfax and Jack L. Roach, eds. *Radical Sociology,* New York: Basic Books.

BENTON, Ted (1984). *The Rise and Fall of Structural Marxism.* New York: St. Martin's Press.

BERNAL, J. D. (1939). *The Social Function of Science.* New York: Macmillan.

BERTAUX, Daniel (1976). *Histoire de vie ou récite de pratiques; méthodologie de l'approche biographique en sociologie.* Paris: Convention Cordes.

BIERSTEDT, Robert (1959). "Nominal and Real Definitions in Sociological Theory," in L. Gross, ed. *Symposium in Sociological Theory.* New York: Harper and Row.

BINNS, Peter (1973). "The Marxist Theory of Truth," *Radical Philosophy.* 4 (Spring):3–9.

BIRNBAUM, Norman (1971). *Toward a Critical Sociology.* New York: Oxford University Press.

BLACKBURN, Robin, and Gareth Stedman Jones (1972). "Louis Althusser and the Struggle for Marxism," in Dick Howard and Karl Klare, eds. *The Unknown Dimension*, New York: Basic Books.

BLALOCK, Hubert M. (1968). "Theory-Building and Causal Inferences," in Ann Blalock and Hubert Blalock, eds. *Methodology in Social Research*. New York: McGraw-Hill.

BLAUBERG, Igor (1977). "The History of Science and the Systems Approach," *Social Sciences*, 8 (3):90–100.

BLAUBERG, I. V., V. N. Sadovsky, and E. G. Yudin (1977). *Systems Theory, Philosophical and Methodological Problems*. Moscow: Progress Publishers.

BLEICHER, Josef (1980). *Contemporary Hermeneutics*. London: Routledge and Kegan Paul.

BLOCH, Ernst (1961). *Philosophische Grundragen* I. Frankfurt: Suhrkamp.

BODEMANN, Michael (1979). "The Fulfillment of Fieldwork in Marxist Practice," *Dialectical Anthropology*, 4:151–61.

BODEMANN, Y. Michael (1978). "A Problem of Sociological Praxis," *Theory and Society*, 5:387–420.

BODINGTON, Stephen (1973). *Computers and Socialism*. Nottingham: Bertrand Russell Peace Foundation.

BOTTOMORE, Thomas H. (1968). "Marxisme et sociologie," *L'homme et la société*, 10:5–11.

BOTTOMORE, Thomas H. (1975). "Competing Paradigms in Macrosociology," in Alex Inkeles, et al., eds. *Annual Review of Sociology*, 1:191–202.

BOTTOMORE, Thomas H. (1978). "Introduction," in T. Bottomore and P. Goode, eds. *Austro-Marxism*. Oxford: Clarendon Press.

BOTTOMORE, Thomas H. (1983). *Dictionary of Marxist Thought*. Oxford: Blackwell.

BOTTOMORE, Thomas H., and Patrick Goode, eds. (1978). *Austro-Marxism*. Oxford: Clarendon Press.

BREINES, Paul (1972). "Praxis and Its Theories: The Import of Lukács and Korsch in the 1920's," *Telos*, 11:67–103.

BRITVIN, V. G. (1980–81). "Sociological Services to Enterprises and Problems of Improving the Effectiveness of Sociological Research," *Soviet Sociology*, 19:58–73.

BRUYN, S. T. (1966). *The Human Perspective in Sociology, the Methodology of Participant Observation*. Englewood Cliffs, N.J.: Prentice-Hall.

BUKHARIN, Nikolai I. (1925). *Historical Materialism: A System of Sociology*. New York: International Publishers.

BUNGE, Mario (1959). *Causality and Modern Science*. New York: Dover Publications.

BURRELL, Gibson, and Gareth Morgan (1979). *Sociological Paradigms and Organisational Analysis*. London: Heinemann.

BURRIS, Val (1979a). "Class and Politics in Advanced Capitalism," *Socialist Review*, 9:135–42.

BURRIS, Val (1979b). "Introduction: The Structuralist Influence in Marxist Theory and Research," *Insurgent Sociologist*, 9:4–17.

CALLINICOS, Alex (1976). *Althusser's Marxism*. London: Pluto Press.

CASTELLS, Manuel, and Emileo de Ipola (1976). "Epistemological Practice and the Social Sciences," *Economy and Society*, 5:111–44.

CATANI, Maurizio (1978). "Susciter une histoire de vie sociale est d'abord affaire de relation" (Creating a Social Life History Is Primarily a Question of Relations). Paper presented at the 9th World Congress of Sociology, Uppsala, Sweden, August 14–18.

CELSO, Ghini (1975). *Il voto degli italiani* (The Italians' Vote). Rome: Editions Riuniti.

COHEN, Stephen, ed. (1982). *An End to Silence: Uncensored Opinion in the Soviet Union*. New York: Norton and Company.

COLFAX, J. David (1970). "Knowledge for Whom?" *Sociological Inquiry*, 40:73–83.

COLLIER, Andrew (1973). "Truth and Practice," *Radical Philosophy*, 5:9–16.

COLLINS, Joseph (1982). *What Difference Could a Revolution Make?; Food and Farming in the New Nicaragua*. San Francisco: Institute for Food and Development Policy.

COMSTOCK, Donald (1980). "A Method for Critical Research: Investigating the World to Change It," Livermore, Colorado: Red Feather Institute for Advanced Studies in Sociology.

CORNFORTH, Maurice (1955a). *Dialectical Materialism: Materialism and the Dialectical Method*. vol. 1. London: Lawrence and Wishart. Second (revised) edition first published in 1952.

CORNFORTH, Maurice (1955b). *Science Versus Idealism: In Defense of Philosophy Against Positivism and Pragmatism*. London: Lawrence and Wishart.

CORNFORTH, Maurice (1963). *Dialectical Materialism: Theory of Knowledge*, vol. 3. London: Lawrence and Wishart. Third revised edition.

CORNFORTH, Maurice (1969). *Dialectical Materialism: Historical Materialism*, vol. 2. London: Lawrence and Wishart. Second (revised) edition first published in 1962.

CROCKER, David (n.d.). "Markovic on Marxian Methodology," Livermore, Colorado: Red Feather Institute for Advanced Studies in Sociology.

CUNNINGHAM, Frank (1973a). *Objectivity in Social Science*. Toronto: University of Toronto Press.

CUNNINGHAM, Frank (1973b). "Practice and Some Muddles About the

Methodology of Historical Materialism," *Canadian Journal of Philosophy*, 3:235–42.

CUNNINGHAM, Frank (1975). "Marxism and Social Science," *Communist Viewpoint*, 7:37–44.

CUNNINGHAM, Frank (1977). "Book Review," in *Science and Society*, 41 (1):107–10.

DENITCH, Bogdan (1971). "Sociology in Eastern Europe: Trends and Prospects," *Slavic Review*, 30 (2):317–39.

EDWARDS, Richard (1979). *Contested Terrain, the Transformation of the Workplace in the Twentieth Century*. New York: Basic Books.

ELZINGA, Aant (1977–78). *Red or Expert: Working Notes on Theory of Science Seen in the Light of the Chinese Revolutionary Experience and Chinese Science Policy Debate*. Gothenberg, Sweden: Institute for Theory of Science, University of Gothenburg. Three volumes.

ENGELS, Frederick (1969). *The Condition of the Working Class in England*. London: Cox and Wyman.

ERLICH, Carol (1976). "The Conditions of Feminist Research," Research Group One, Report 21, February, 2743 Maryland Ave., Baltimore, Md. 21218.

FEDOSEYEV, Pyotr (1983). "The Unity of the Natural and Social Sciences and Their Interaction," *Social Sciences*, 14 (2):14–26.

FISCHER, George (1966). "Current Soviet Work in Sociology," *American Sociologist* (May) 127–32.

FLACKS, Richard, and Gerald Turkel (1978). "Radical Sociology: The Emergence of Neo-Marxism Perspectives in U.S. Sociology," *Annual Review of Sociology*, 4:193–238.

FOUCAULT, Michel (1971). *L'ordre du discours* (Orders of discourse). Paris: Gallimard.

FOUCAULT, Michel (1972). *The Archaeology of Knowledge*. New York: Pantheon Books.

FOUCAULT, Michel (1976). *La Volonté de savoir* (The will to knowledge). Paris: Gallimard.

FREIRE, Paulo (1972). "Une orientation: méthode de recherche" (An orientation: research methods). Extracts from a presentation to a conference on the study of adult education, Dar-es-Salaam: July 20.

FREUND, Peter, and Mona Abrams (1976). "Ethnomethodology and Marxism: Their Use for Critical Theorizing," *Theory and Society*, 3:377–93.

FRITZHAND, Marek (1966). "Marx's Ideal Man," in Erich Fromm, ed. *Socialist Humanism*, New York: Doubleday.

GALTUNG, Johan (1977). *Methodology and Ideology*. Copenhagen: Christian Ejlers.

GERDES, Paulus (1985). *Demystifying Calculus: On the Significance of*

*Marx's Mathematical Manuscripts.* Minneapolis, Minn.: Marxist Educational Press (MEP).

GOODE, Patrick (1979). *Karl Korsch: A Study in Western Marxism.* London: Macmillan.

GORMAN, Robert A. (1982). *Neo-Marxism: The Meaning of Modern Radicalism.* Westport, Conn.: Greenwood Press.

GOULDNER, Alvin (1970). *The Coming Crisis of Western Sociology.* New York: Avon.

GRAHAM, Loren R. (1964). "Cybernetics in the Soviet Union," *Surveys, A Journal of Soviet and East European Studies.* 52 (July):3–18.

GRAHAM, Loren R. (1972). *Science and Philosophy in the Soviet Union.* New York: Alfred A. Knopf.

GRAHAM, Loren R. (1981). *Between Science and Values.* New York: Columbia University Press.

GRAMSCI, Antonio (1971). *Selections from the Prison Notebooks.* Q. Hoare and G. Nowell, trans. New York: International Publishers.

GRIFFITHS, Dot, John Irvine, and Ian Miles (1979). "Social Statistics: Toward a Radical Science," in John Irvine, Ian Miles, and Jeff Evans, eds. *Demystifying Social Statistics.* London: Pluto Press.

GURVITCH, G. (1953). "L'hyper-empirisme dialectique, ses applications en sociologie" (Dialectical hyper-empiricism: its applications to sociology), *Cahier international de sociologie,* 15:3–33.

HABERMAS, Jürgen (1968). *Knowledge and Human Interests.* Boston: Beacon Press.

HAHN, Jeffrey W. (1977). "The Role of Soviet Sociologists in the Making of Social Policy," in Richard B. Remnek, ed. *Social Scientists and Policy Making in the USSR.* New York: Praeger Publishers.

HAHN, Werner G. (1982). *Post War Soviet Politics: The Fall of Zhdanov and the Defeat of Moderation 1946–53.* Ithaca, N.Y.: Cornell University Press.

HARVEY, David (1973). *Social Justice and the City.* Bungay, Suffolk: Edward Arnold.

HEIPLE, Phil, and Richard Pozzuto (1975). "Gramsci on Blalock," Livermore, Colorado: Red Feather Institute for Advanced Studies in Sociology.

HEISE, D. R. (1970). "Causal Inference from Panel Data," in E. E. Borgatta and G. W. Bohrnstedt, eds. *Sociological Methodology.* San Francisco: Jossey-Bass.

HINDESS, Barry, and Paul Hirst (1975). *Pre-Capitalist Modes of Production.* London: Routledge and Kegan Paul.

HORKHEIMER, Max (1972). "Traditional and Critical Theory," in M. J. O'Connell, trans. *Critical Theory: Selected Essays.* New York: Herder and Herder.

HORKHEIMER, Max, and Theodor Adorno (1972). *Dialectic of Enlightenment*. New York: Herder and Herder.

HORTON, John (1972). "Combatting Empiricism: Toward a Practical Understanding of Marxist Methodology," *Insurgent Sociologist*, 3 (Fall):24–34.

HORTON, John, and Fari Filsoufi (1977). "Left-Wing Communism: An Infantile Disorder in Theory and Method," *Insurgent Sociologist*, 7 (Winter):5–11.

HOWARD, Michael, and John E. King (1975). *The Political Economy of Marx*. Essex: Longman.

IADOV, V. A. (1975). "Some Problems in the Theory of and General Approach to Sociological Research" (Part I and Part II), *Soviet Sociology*, 14 (1):3–32, (3):3–25.

INSTITUTE OF SOCIAL RESEARCH (1981). *Newsletter*, 19 (Summer).

IRVINE, John, Ian Miles, and Jeff Evans (1979). "Introduction," in John Irvine, Ian Miles, and Jeff Evans, eds. *Demystifying Social Statistics*. London: Pluto Press.

ISRAEL, Joachim (1971). "The Principle of Methodological Individualism and Marxian Epistemology," *Acta Sociologica*, 14 (3):145–50.

JORAVSKY, David (1961). *Soviet Marxism and Natural Science, 1917–32*. London: Routledge and Kegan Paul.

KALÀB, Milŏs (1969a). "The Marxist Conception of the Sociological Method," *Quality and Quantity*, 3 (January):5–22.

KALÀB, Milŏs (1969b). "The Specificity of the Marxist Conception of Sociology," in Peter Berger, ed. *Marxism and Sociology*. New York: Appleton-Century-Crofts.

KAMENKA, Eugene (1966). "Marxian Humanism and the Crisis in Socialist Ethics," in Erich Fromm, ed. *Socialist Humanism*. New York: Doubleday.

KAMENKA, Eugene (1969). "Soviet Philosophy 1917–1967," in Alex Simirenko, ed. *Social Thought in the Soviet Union*. Chicago: Quadrangle Books.

KARMEN, Andrew (1972). "Dialectics Versus Path Analysis," *The Human Factor*, 11 (1):22–31.

KEDROV, B., and A. Spirkin (1975). "Science," in T. J. Blakeley, ed. *Themes in Soviet Marxist Philosophy*. Dordrecht, Holland: D. Reidel Publishing.

KELLE, V., and N. Makeshin (1977–79). "Sociological Problems of Research into Relationships and Activities in the Sphere of Science," *Problems of the Science of Science* (4–5).

KELLEY, Donald R. (1977). "Group and Specialist Influence in Soviet Politics: In Search of a Theory," in Richard B. Remnek, ed. *Social Scientists and Policy Making in the USSR*. New York: Praeger Publishers.

KESSELMAN, Mark (1983). "From State Theory to Class Struggle and Compromise: Contemporary Marxist Political Studies," *Social Science Quarterly*, 69 (4):826–45.

KOHLI, Martin (1978). "Biographical Method—Methodological Biography?" Paper presented to the 9th World Congress of Sociology, Uppsala, Sweden, August 14–18.

KOLAKOWSKI, Leszek (1968). *Toward a Marxist Humanism*. New York: Grove Press.

KOLAKOWSKI, Leszek (1972). *Positivist Philosophy from Hume to the Vienna Circle*. Harmondsworth, England: Penguin.

KOLAKOWSKI, Leszek (1978a). *Main Currents of Marxism*, vol. 1. Oxford: Clarendon Press.

KOLAKOWSKI, Leszek (1978b). *Main Currents of Marxism*, vol. 2. Oxford: Clarendon Press.

KOLAKOWSKI, Leszek (1978c). *Main Currents of Marxism*, vol. 3. Oxford: Clarendon Press.

KOSIK, Karel (1976). *The Dialectics of the Concrete*. Boston: D. Reidel Publishers.

KOZLOVSKII, V. E., and Iu A. Sychev (1970–71). "Discussion of Iu A. Levada's Course of Lectures on Sociology." *Soviet Sociology*, 9:475–94.

KUZMIN, Vsevolod (1979). "Systems Foundations and Structures in Marx's Methodology," *Social Sciences*, 10 (1):45–64.

LACOSTE-DUJARDIN, Camille (1977). "La relation d'enquête" (The relation of inquiry), *Herodote*, 8:21–44.

LANE, David (1970). "Ideology and Sociology in the U.S.S.R.," *The British Journal of Sociology*, 21 (1):43–51.

LARIONOV, M. P. (1970). "On Methods and Methodology of Social Research in the Works of Lenin," *Soviet Studies in Philosophy*, 19 (Summer):81–96.

LARRAIN, Jorge (1979). *The Concept of Ideology*. Athens: University of Georgia Press.

LAURENT, Paul (1979). "A l'image de ceux qui luttent" (In the image of those who struggle), *L'Humanité*, Saturday 28, April.

LAVIGNE, M. (1968). "Les sciences humaines dans la recherche en Union Soviétique" (The human sciences in research in the Soviet Union), *Annuaire de l'URSS/annuaire de l'URSS et des pays socialistes Européens*, 779–849.

LAZARSFELD, Paul F. (1972). *Qualitative Analysis*. Boston: Allyn and Bacon, Inc.

LECOURT, Dominique (1975). *Marxism and Epistemology*. London: New Left Books.

LECOURT, Dominique (1977). *Proletarian Science: The Case of Lysenko*. London: New Left Books.

LEE, Alfred McClung (1975). "Humanist Challenges to Positivists," *The Insurgent Sociologist*, 6 (Fall):41–52.

LEFEBVRE, Henri (1969a). *The Sociology of Marx.* Norbert Guterman, trans. New York: Random House.

LEFEBVRE, Henri (1969b). *Logique formelle, logique dialectique.* Paris: Anthropos.

LEFEBVRE, Henri (1970). *La révolution urbaine.* Paris: Gallimard.

LEITER, Kenneth (1980). *A Primer on Ethnomethodology.* New York: Oxford University Press.

LEKTORSKY, Vladislaw, and Serafim Melyukhin (1977). "Trends in the Development of Materialist Dialectics," *Social Sciences*, 1:75–84.

LENIN, V. I. (1956). *The Development of Capitalism in Russia.* Moscow: Foreign Languages Publishing House.

LENIN, V. I. (1964). "Statistics and Sociology," in *Collected Works*, vol. 23. Moscow: Progress Publishers.

LENIN, V. I. (1972). "Conspectus of Hegel's Book *The Science of Logic*," *Collected Works*, vol. 38. Moscow: Progress Publishers.

LEON, Victor (1971). "Les Sciences sociales en Europe de l'Est," *Revue de l'Est* 2 (3):155–71.

LEWIN, Moshe (1974). *Political Undercurrents in Soviet Economic Debates: From Bukharin to the Modern Reforms.* Princeton, N.J.: Princeton University Press.

LEWIS, John (1955). *Marxism and the Irrationalists.* Westport, Conn.: Greenwood Press.

LEWONTIN, Richard, and Richard Levins (1976). "The Problem of Lysenkoism," in Hilary Rose and Steven Rose, eds. *The Radicalisation of Science.* London: Macmillan.

LOJKINE, Jean (1977). *Le Marxisme, l'gétat, et la question urbaine* (Marxism, the state and the urban question). Paris: PUF.

LOVELL, Terry (1980). *Pictures of Reality Aesthetics, Politics, Pleasure.* London: British Film Institute.

LOWY, Michael (1973). *Dialectique et Règolution* (Dialectic and revolution). Paris: Anthropos.

LUKACS, Georg (1971). *History and Class Consciousness.* London: Merlin Press.

LYSMANKIN, E. (1977). "The Methodology of Social Sciences," *Social Sciences*, 8 (4):210–13.

MACCIOCCHI, Maria Antonietta (1969). *Letters from Inside the Italian Communist Party to Louis Althusser.* London: New Left Books.

McINNES, Neil (1972). *The Western Marxists.* New York: Library Press.

McLELLAN, David (1975). *Marx.* London: Fontana.

McQUARIE, Donald (1976). "Central Problems in Karl Marx's Sociology," *Sociological Analysis and Theory*, 6: 211–40.

McQUARIE, Donald (1978). "Marx and the Method of Successive Approximations," *The Sociological Quarterly*, 9 (Spring):218–33.

MANDIC, Oleg (1967). "The Marxist School of Sociology: What Is Sociology in a Marxist Sense?" *Social Research* (Autumn):435–55.

MANNHEIMER, R., M. Rodriguez, and C. Sebastiani (1979). *Gli operai comunisti* (Communist Workers). Rome: Editions Riuniti.

MAO Zedong (1966). *On Practice*. Peking: Foreign Languages Press.

MAO Zedong (1971). *Selected Readings from the Works of Mao Tsetung*. Peking: Foreign Languages Press.

MARCUSE, Herbert (1956). *Reason and Revolution*. New York: Humanities Press.

MARCUSE, Herbert (1967). *One Dimensional Man*. Boston: Beacon Press.

MARCUSE, Herbert (1969). *Negations: Essays in Critical Theory*. Boston: Beacon Press.

MARKOVIC, Mihailo (1974). *From Affluence to Praxis*. Ann Arbor, Mich.: Ann Arbor Press.

MARQUIT, Erwin (1977). "Statistical Process and Causality," *Revolutionary World*, 21–25:171–79.

MARX, Karl (1880). "Enquête ouvrière," *Revue Socialiste*, 4, 20 April 1880:193–99. Reprinted in *Karl Marx: Selected Writings in Sociology and Social Philosophy*. T. B. Bottomore, trans. New York: McGraw-Hill, 1956.

MARX, Karl (1973). *Grundrisse*. Martin Nicolaus, trans. and ed. New York: Vintage Books.

MATTHEWS, Mervyn (1978). *Soviet Sociology, 1964–1975*. New York: Praeger Publishers.

MEDVEDEV, Zhores (1969). *The Rise and Fall of T. D. Lysenko*. New York: Columbia University Press.

MEEHAN, Eugene (1981). *Reasoned Argument in Social Science*. Westport, Conn.: Greenwood Press.

MEEHAN, Eugene (1982). *Economics and Policymaking*. Westport, Conn.: Greenwood Press.

MEEHAN, Eugene (1986). "Policy: Constructing a Definition," *Policy Sciences*, forthcoming.

MESZAROS, I. (1972). *Lukacs' Concept of the Dialectic*. London: Merlin Press.

MEUNIER, Jean-Guy (1973). "Le matérialisme dialectique, cahier guide pour le cours PHI–341." Montréal: Université du Québec á Montréal, Département de Philosophie.

MILIBAND, Ralph (1969). *The State in Capitalist Society*. New York: Basic Books.

MILLS, C. Wright (1962). *The Marxists*. New York: Dell.

MORGAN, George Allen (1966). "Stalin on Revolution," in Alex Simirenko, ed. *Soviet Sociology*. Chicago: Quadrangle Books.

MSHVENIERADZE, V. V., and G. V. Osipov (1966). "The Principal Trends and Subject Matter of Concrete Sociological Research," *Soviet Sociology*, 5 (1) (Summer) :13–21.

NALETOV, Igor (1984). *Alternatives to Positivism*. Moscow: Progress Publishers.

NIELSEN, Kai (1972). "Is Empiricism an Ideology?" *Metaphilosophy*, 3 (October): 265–73.

O'CONNOR, James (1973). *The Fiscal Crisis of the State*. New York: St. Martin's Press.

OIZERMAN, Theodore (1975). "Epistemological Analysis of Categories in Lenin's Works," *Social Sciences*, 6 (1): 52–64.

OSIPOV, G., and M. Yovchuk (1963). "Some Principles of Theory, Problems, and Methods of Research in Sociology in the USSR." *American Sociological Review* 28 (4):620–23.

OSIPOVA, Elena V. (1971). "Soviet Union," in Jerzy Wiatr, ed. *The State of Sociology in Eastern Europe Today*. Carbondale: Southern Illinois University Press.

OSSOWSKI, Stanislav (1962). "W Sprawie Badan Ankietowych" (Pertaining to Questionnaire Research), *Polityka*, 2:12.

PALMER, Bryan D. (1981). *The Making of E. P. Thompson*. Toronto: New Hogtown Press.

PAPINEAU, David (1978). *For Science in the Social Sciences*. London: Macmillan.

PAREKH, Bhikhu (1982). *Marx's Theory of Ideology*. Baltimore: Johns Hopkins University Press.

PARSONS, Talcott (1965). "An American Impression of Sociology in the Soviet Union," *American Sociological Review*, (30):121–25.

PECHEUX, Michel (1975). *Les vérités de la palice*. Paris: Maspero.

PICCONE, Paul (1971). "Phenomenological Marxism," *Telos*, 9:3–31.

PILSWORTH, Michael, and Ralph Ruddock (1975). "Some Criticisms of Survey Research," *Convergence*, 8 (2):33–43.

POULANTZAS, Nicos (1973). *Political Power and Social Classes*. London: New Left Books.

POULANTZAS, Nicos (1978). *Classes in Contemporary Capitalism*. London: New Left Books.

POZZUTO, Richard (1973). "Pre-Marxian Marxism: A Critique of Szymanski's Marxism and Science," *Insurgent Sociologist*, 3 (Summer):48–55.

PUSHKIN, V. (1980). "Reviews," *Social Sciences*, 11 (2):271–74.

RICHTA, Radovan, et al. (1968). *Civilization at the Crossroads: Social and Human Implications of the Scientific and Technological Revolution*. 3rd edition. New York: International Arts and Sciences Press Inc.

ROSE, Hilary, and Steven Rose eds. (1976). *The Political Economy of Science: Ideology of/in the Natural Sciences*. London: Macmillan.

ROSSMAN, Edwin (1981). "Empirical Imperatives of Marxian Sociology," *Free Inquiry in Creative Sociology*, 9 (2):145–48.

ROUMIANTSEV, A. M., and G. B. Ossipov (1969). "La Sociologie marxiste et les recherches empiriques," *L'homme et la société* (October-December):92–112.

SARTRE, Jean-Paul (1963). *Search for a Method*. New York: Alfred A. Knopf.

SCHAFF, Adam (1971). *Histoire et vérité*. Paris: Anthropos.

SCHWARTZ, Donald V. (1973). "Recent Soviet Adaptations of Systems Theory to Administrative Theory," *Journal of Comparative Administration*, 5 (2):233–64.

SEKINE, Thomas (1980). "An Essay on Uno's Dialectic of Capital," in Kozo Uno, ed. *Principles of Political Economy, Theory of a Purely Capitalist Society*. Atlantic Highlands, N.J.: Humanities.

SEUNG, T. K. (1982). *Structuralism and Hermeneutics*. New York: Columbia University Press.

SHALIN, Dmitri N. (1978). "The Development of Soviet Sociology 1956–76," in Ralph Turner, et al., eds. *Annual Review of Sociology*. Palo Alto, Calif.: Annual Review, Inc.

SHERMAN, Howard (1976). "Dialectics As a Method," *Insurgent Sociologist*, 6 (4):57–64.

SIU-LUN WONG (1979). *Sociology and Socialism in Contemporary China*. London: Routledge and Kegan Paul.

SLIDER, Darrell (1985). "Party Sponsored Public Opinion in the Soviet Union," *Journal of Politics*, 47 (February):209–27.

SMOLICZ, J. J. (1974). "Some Impressions of Polish Sociology," *The Australian and New Zealand Journal of Sociology*, 10 (1):17–25.

SOCIAL SCIENCE RESEARCH COUNCIL (1979). *Items* (June).

SOLOMON, Peter H., Jr. (1977). "Specialists in Soviet Policy Making: Criminal Policy 1938–1970," in Richard S. Remnek, ed. *Social Scientists and Policy Making in the USSR*. New York: Praeger Publishers.

SOMERVILLE, John (1967). *The Philosophy of Marxism*. New York: Random House.

SPADIJER, Balsa (1979). "La science politique: théorie et pratique yougoslaves" (Political science: Yugoslavian theory and practice), *Revue international des sciences sociales*. Paris: UNESCO, 31 (1):136–42.

SPIRKIN, A. (1975). "Dialectical Materialism," in T. J. Blakeley, ed. *Themes in Soviet Marxist Philosophy*. Dordrecht, Holland: D. Reidel Publishing Company.

STALIN, Joseph V. (1972). *Economic Problems of Socialism in the USSR*. Peking: Foreign Languages Press.

STAVENHAGEN, Rodolfo (1971). "Comment decoloniser les sciences sociales appliquées" (How to decolonize the applied social sciences), *Les temps modernes*, 27:2362–86.

SZACKI, Jerzy (1979). *History of Sociological Thought*. Westport, Conn.: Greenwood Press.

SZCZEPANSKI, Jan (1966). "Sociologie Marxiste empirique," *L'homme et la société*, 1 (July):45–53.

SZTOMPKA, Piotr (1979a). *Sociological Dilemmas Toward a Dialectic Paradigm*. New York: Academic Press.

SZTOMPKA, Piotr (1979b). "Marxism, Functionalism and Systems Approach," in Jerzy Wiatr, ed. *Polish Essays in the Methodology of the Social Science*. Boston: D. Reidel Publishing Company.

SZYMANSKI, Albert (1973). "Marxism and Science," *Insurgent Socialist*, 3 (Summer):25–38.

THERBORN, Göran (1976). *Science, Class and Society*. London: New Left Books.

THOMAS, James (1977). "Marx, Hegel and Dialectical Method," *Insurgent Sociologist*, 7:49–55.

THOMPSON, E. P. (1978). *The Poverty of Theory and Other Essays*. New York: Monthly Review Press.

THOMPSON, Paul P. (1978). *The Voice of the Past: Oral History*. New York: Oxford University Press.

TIMPANARO, Sebastiano (1975). *On Materialism*, Lawrence Garner, trans. London: New Left Books.

UKRAINTSEV, Boris (1978). "Marxism-Leninism and Social Science Methods," *Social Sciences*, 9 (3):90–103.

VAILLANCOURT, Pauline (1979). "Le marxisme empirique dans les pays de l'Ouest" (Empirical Marxism in Western countries), *Les cahiers du socialisme*, 4 (Fall):108–79.

VAILLANCOURT, Pauline (1986). "Nicaragua: An Experiment in Revolutionary Pluralism" in *Socialism and the Future*, ed. Toronto: Between the Lines.

VAN DEN BERG, Axel (1980). "Critical Theory: Is There Still Hope?" *American Journal of Sociology*, 86 (3):449–78.

VANEAU, François (1979). "La société devant l'informatique" (Society faces computer science), *Humanité* 3 April:2.

VERRET, Michel (1979). "L'Ouvrier français: l'espace ouvrier" (The French worker: worker space). Paris: Armand Colin.

VERRET, Michel (1982). "L'Ouvrier français: le travail ouvrier" (The French worker: worker labor). Paris: Armand Colin.

VAN STEENBERGEN, Bart (1970). "Critical and Establishment Futurology," in *Challenge from the Future, Proceedings of the International Future Research Conference*, vol. 1. Tokyo: Kodansha.

WEINBERG, Elizabeth Ann (1974). *The Development of Sociology in the Soviet Union*. London and Boston: Routledge and Kegan Paul.

WELSH, William, ed. (1981). *Survey Research and Public Attitudes in Eastern Europe and the Soviet Union.* New York: Pergamon Press.

WETTER, Gustav (1964). *Dialectical Materialism.* London: Routledge and Kegan.

WIATR, Jerzy (1979). *Polish Essays in the Methodology of the Social Sciences.* Boston: D. Reidel Publishing Company.

WRIGHT, Erik Olin (1978). *Class, Crisis and the State.* London: New Left Books.

WRIGHT, Erik Olin (1979). *Class Structure and Income Determination.* New York: Academic Press.

YOUNG, Bob (1977). "Science Is Social Relations," *Radical Science Journal,* 5:65–129.

YOUNG, T. R., Richard B. Hovard, and Robert Christie (1977). "Conflict Moments in Critical Methodology," Livermore, Colorado: Red Feather Institute for Advanced Studies in Sociology.

YOUNG, T. R. (1977). "Criticism and Self-Criticism: Theory and Practice for Marxist Social Science." Livermore, Colorado: Red Feather Institute for Advanced Studies in Sociology.

ZAHAVI, Uri (1973). "Karl Korsch and the Western School of Marxism," *Social Praxis,* 1:185–202.

ZDRAVOMYSLOV, A. G., and V. A. Iadov (1966). "Soviet Workers' Attitudes Toward Work," in Alex Simirenko, ed. *Soviet Sociology.* Chicago: Quadrangle Books.

ZELENY, Jindvich (1980). *The Logic of Marx.* Terrell Carver, ed. and trans. Oxford: Basil Blackwell.

ZIVKOVIC, Ljubomir (1969). "Structure of Marxist Sociology," in Peter Berger, ed. *Marxism and Sociology.* New York: Appleton-Century-Crofts.

# INDEX

## About the Author

PAULINE MARIE VAILLANCOURT is Professor of Political Science at the University of Quebec at Montreal. Her articles have appeared, in both French and English, in numerous publications, among them *Public Opinion Quarterly, The Journal of Social and Behavioral Science, Our Generation, Working Teacher*, and *Canadian Dimension*.